# Ducks

# Ducks

*Tending a Small-Scale Flock for Pleasure and Profit*

BY CHERIE LANGLOIS

HOBBY H F FARM PRESS®

An Imprint of BowTie Press®
A Division of BowTie, Inc.
Irvine, California

June Kikuchi, *Editorial Director*
Jarelle S. Stein, *Editor*
Karen Julian, *Publishing Coordinator*
Tracy Burns, Jessica Jaensch, *Production Coordinators*
Lisa Barfield, *Book Design Concept*
Joe Bernier, *Book Design and Layout*
Indexed by Melody Englund

Library of Congress Cataloging-in-Publication Data

Langlois, Cherie.
  Ducks : tending a small-scale flock for pleasure and profit / by Cherie Langlois.
      p. cm. — (Hobby farms)
  Includes bibliographical references and index.
  ISBN 978-1-933958-16-3
  1. Ducks.  I. Title. II. Series.

  SF505.L36 2008
  636.5'97—dc22

                                                                                    2007020573

BowTie Press®
A Division of BowTie, Inc.
3 Burroughs
Irvine, California 92618

Printed and bound in China
13  12  11  10  09      4  5  6  7  8  9  10

In memory of Nana, who always believed I'd be a writer, and for my parents, who encouraged my love of animals.

# Table of Contents

# Why Ducks?

Well, why not ducks? Whereas in the United States, the domestic duck still waddles about in the shadow of the immensely popular chicken, in other parts of the world—especially Asia—ducks are just as important as chickens in the lives and diets of humans. What do these water-crazy birds have that make them as much an asset to farms as landlubbing poultry? For starters, ducks are one of the hardiest, most efficient foragers out there—even more so than their clucky cousins. Properly tended, these birds seldom get sick. Given some freedom to roam pasture, pond, or orchard, they'll glean much of their own feed. Of course, you're welcome to spoil them if you want to, but a small duck flock doesn't have to be babied with elaborate, heated accommodations. Do you live in the frigid North? Lack a pond on your property? Work full time? Not a problem! Ducks will adapt to a wide range of climates and living conditions and thrive on a minimum of daily care as long as you meet their basic needs, as outlined in this book.

In return, ducks are generous, industrious creatures. Like chickens, ducks on the prowl for their chow provide valuable pest control, weeding, and fertilization services. They efficiently convert food sources into protein-packed meat and eggs, and they give us dreamy-soft duck down for pillows and comforters. Colorful and personable, ducks favor us with intangible gifts as well. They make lovely exhibition fowl and gentle, endlessly amusing, interesting pets. Given access to any body of water, big or little, they flap their wings, dunk their heads, and splash like playful, happy kids forever on summer break.

If you think you might like to add splash and sparkle to your farm with domestic ducks, this book will give you the information you need to get started.

# CHAPTER ONE

# Meet the Duck

A ll birds—including the captivating duck— possess adaptations that set them apart from most other backboned animals, or vertebrates. Of course, the unique avian characteristic that attracts and delights us most of all must surely be feathers! What else gives these animals their eye-popping range of colors and contributes so much to their enviable power of flight? But birds have more going for them than just feathers (we'll talk about plumage in a bit); they've evolved some other interesting and useful features you should know about, too.

## HOW BIRDS ARE BUILT

The wild ducks from which our domestic duck breeds descend can fly fast, far, and high, thanks to a number of specialized adaptations. A flying bird's skeleton is light and strong, consisting of thin, often air-filled, or pneumatic, bones. The bones that make up the wings evolved from the forelimbs of the birds' dinosaur ancestor (some bones being fused and some eliminated down through the ages). The breastbone has a large protrusion called a keel, to which the highly developed wing muscles attach. Most birds have more cervical vertebrae than other vertebrates do, and if you've ever seen a duck preen or a swan arch its graceful neck, you know that most birds also have neck bones far more flexible than ours.

Unlike us, birds have no teeth; the avian jaw is narrow and elongated, forming a horn-covered, toothless beak. Birds' beaks vary in shape and size—with outlandish effect, in some cases!—each type adapted to handling the specific foods in the species' diet. In most birds, food travels down the esophagus and enters a handy, expandable storage chamber called a crop. From there, it moves into a stomach consisting of two chambers: the proventriculus, which secretes gastric juice as does the human stomach, and the muscular gizzard. Standing in for teeth, the gizzard grinds seeds, grains, insects, and other foods with the help of ingested stone particles called grit, which the bird picks up as it forages. Avian digestive, urinary, and reproductive systems all terminate in one chamber, known as the cloaca, where urine and fecal material mix together and then exit the body via the vent. As we all know, birds reproduce by laying eggs, a characteristic they share with reptiles and their dinosaur ancestors.

In general, birds have terrific eyesight. The duck, for example, sees colors, and each of its eyes has a visual field of over 180 degrees, giving it binocular

## Did You Know?

Birds have a poor sense of taste. A Mallard has only about 375 taste buds, while we humans possess a whopping 9,000 to 10,000. No wonder they like slugs! But wait—pigeons have even fewer taste buds than ducks have. Anybody care for a stale bread crumb? Bon appétit!

vision to the front, to the rear, and even overhead—a huge plus for spotting sneaky predators. Birds' hearing is also well developed, but their sense of taste is poor, and with the exception of some species, such as vultures, so is their sense of smell.

Birds have a rapid heart rate, a high metabolism, and an active lifestyle that requires them to consume plenty of food

*Birds delight us with their gorgeous variety of colors. The metallic green-blue sheen of this Muscovy duck's feathers stems from their light-absorbing and light-reflecting surface structure.*

(so much for eating like a bird!). Avian body weights range from a fraction of an ounce (the bee hummingbird) to more than 300 pounds (the ostrich). A bird's compact lungs connect to air sacs that branch out through its body, an amazingly efficient respiratory system that allows a migrating swan to fly at 20,000 feet in altitude and a Ruby-Throated Hummingbird to beat its wings up to seventy times a second. This efficient respiratory system, along with a high metabolism, also accounts for birds' extreme sensitivity to breathing toxic substances. Birds are so susceptible to toxic gases that historically, coal miners were able to rely on this avian attribute to save their own lives. They took canaries down into the mines with them to serve as an early detection system: the birds'

demise warned them of the presence of deadly gases.

In an eggshell, birds—and our ducks—are feathered, flying, toothless dinosaurs.

## SPECIFIC WATERFOWL TRAITS

Although lots of birds spend time around water, what we normally refer to as waterfowl are swimming game birds in the family Anatidae: ducks and their larger relatives, geese and swans. About 150 species of waterfowl are found throughout the world, occupying every continent except Antarctica. More than fifty of these species inhabit North America, most of them migratory to some degree. In their wild state, these talented birds rule the waters, swimming, diving, and dabbling (that

*Like all swans, this elegant Mute swan belongs to the family Anatidae, which also includes the swan's water-loving relatives, ducks and geese. Birds in this family are often referred to as waterfowl.*

*The Canada goose, a relative of the domestic duck and a common visitor to North American parks and lakes, is just one of approximately 150 species of waterfowl found throughout the world.*

is, feeding in shallow water). But they can fly high in the sky and waddle across land with varying degrees of success as well.

All waterfowl, domestic and wild, share certain important physiological traits and behaviors. Here's a speedy overview of the ones that will help you better understand the domestic duck.

*Using their bills as sifters, a wild Mallard pair dabbles for aquatic insects and plants on a quiet lake.*

## WEBBED FEET AND DUCK BILLS

Look at a Mallard, and you see a bird built for a semiaquatic life. Large webbed feet propel its streamlined body along the surface of lakes and keep it from sinking into the soft mud of marshes and estuaries. Its short legs sit toward the middle of its belly, allowing the duck to walk on land and achieve an explosive takeoff from water. By contrast, a heavier diving duck such as the Merganser has legs situated back near the tail and needs a running start to get airborne.

Now check out that funny-looking bill, yellow in the Mallard male (or drake), orange and black in the female (or duck). Mallards and their domestic descendants are called dabbling ducks or puddle ducks. At times, they submerge themselves completely, but more often, they bob around on top of shallow bodies of water, using their broad bills to dabble for floating plant material, bugs, and mosquito larvae. They also tip tails-up to scrounge around in the mud, sifting out the edibles with their lamellae—comblike plates lining the upper and lower bills. That big bill works on land, too, where the Mallard waddles around using it to tug at tender grass, gobble up berries and seeds, and nab slugs and snails.

## Biological Classification

**Kingdom:** Animalia (animals)
**Phylum:** Chordata (animals with backbones)
**Class:** Aves (birds)
**Order:** Anseriformes (ducks, geese, and swans)
**Family:** Anatidae (ducks, geese, and swans)
**Tribe:** Cairinini (perching ducks) for the Muscovy
Anatini (surface-feeding ducks) for Mallard-derived breeds
**Genus, Species, and Subspecies:** *Cairina moschata* (Muscovy); *Anas platyrhynchos domesticus* (Mallard derivatives )

## FINE FEATHERS

Like our hair, duck feathers and down are made up of dead cells that are pushed up from the epidermis as new cells grow underneath. Composed mainly of a protein called keratin, feathers come in many lovely hues. Two main factors influence plumage color: the type of pigment

National Geographic's *Field Guide to the Birds of North America* divides duck-like waterfowl into the following eight types:

**Whistling Ducks:** Upright and goose-like, these ducks are characterized by their distinctive, high-pitched whistles.

**Perching Ducks:** Perchers like the Muscovy and Wood duck frequent wooded areas, forage on the water surface, and perch in trees.

**Dabbling Ducks:** Dabblers glean food from the surface of shallow bodies of water or by tipping tails-up to snag underwater edibles. Members include the Mallard, the Pintail, and most domestic duck breeds.

**Pochards:** Heavy-bodied diving ducks in this group include the Canvasback and Redhead.

**Eiders:** These big northern ducks have a dense coat of down to keep them warm as they dive for food in the frigid sea.

**Sea Ducks:** This ocean-loving group of divers includes the stocky Surf Scoter and the Harlequin duck.

**Mergansers:** These streamlined waterfowl with thin serrated bills are superb divers and fish catchers.

**Stiff-tailed Ducks:** The only common species of this type in North America, the stocky Ruddy duck uses its stiffly upright tail as a rudder when it dives.

---

deposited during feather development, and the light-reflecting and light-absorbing surface qualities of the feathers.

Adult ducks molt their old, worn feathers—including their flight feathers—once a year as bright new ones gradually come in. This annual casting off of feathers, called the postnuptial molt, normally occurs after the breeding season. During this time, which may last from one to two months, ducks are unable to fly, making them the perfect lunch for a hungry predator. No doubt, this is where the term *sitting duck* originated. For some duck species such as the Mallard, however, nature has pro-

vided an ingenious solution to the problem: as the drakes lose their gaudy feathers in a summer eclipse molt, they take on a camouflaging brown plumage

*This mixed flock of iridescent black Cayugas, white Pekin, and white Muscovies (background) illustrates two extremes of feather coloring in ducks.*

*This once-colorful Mallard drake (in background) has undergone his summer eclipse molt, adopting the drabber coloration of the female Mallard in the foreground. At a time when he's unable to fly and so is more vulnerable to predators, this color change could save his life.*

similar to the females'—a lifesaving adaptation when they're incapable of flying. A second molt during fall returns them to their former dapper selves.

Feathers are vital to a bird. They enable flight, of course, but they also conserve body heat, protect the skin, and help a duck stay afloat by trapping air. Ditto for the soft down that makes ducklings so cute.

To function well, feathers must be kept clean, and ducks need no bribing to take regular baths. While domestic ducks can survive without water to bathe in, they feel and look their best when provided proper bath facilities. Besides, watching waterfowl bathe is one of the chief joys of having them on your farm. They happily dip their heads beneath the water over and over, beating their wings to make a glittering rainbow spray. Ducks know how to have fun!

All birds spend time each day preening their feathers, but for water-loving birds such as ducks, feather preening is much more than just a lengthy beauty routine—it's a matter of life and death. Feathers and down must keep a duck's body warm and dry even when the bird dips for pond plants on a frigid winter day. This means the bird must groom each feather meticulously into place and

*The preening Pekin pair pictured here may look vain, but their meticulous feather grooming has a life-saving purpose: to distribute water-repelling oil and relock feather barbules so their plumage will keep them warm and dry.*

regularly distribute oil from its uropygial gland (or preen gland, as it is also called) over the plumage so it will repel water.

Watch any duck emerge from a bath, and you'll see a whole lot of tail, body, and wing shaking going on. The duck will get busy, scratching at its feathers with its bill and toenails to reposition and relock the barbules and trap in an insulating layer of air; ruffling its feathers to expose the oil gland above the tail; and repeatedly rubbing its head and bill against the gland to release the oil. Then you'll see it distributing this oil throughout the wing and tail feathers by combing them through its bill.

## DUCK BEHAVIOR

Like wolves, bison, and humans, most ducks are social animals. You see them in huge feeding or migrating flocks, courting pairs, or mother-and-duckling families, but you rarely see them alone, except in the case of a duck incubating her eggs.

Flocking behavior has its pros and cons. On the one hand, birds living in a large group are at increased risk of disease. They also run the risk of wiping out their food supply. Another danger is that a quacking, fluttering flock will more likely attract a predator's attention than will a single duck floating quietly among the cattails. On the other hand, individual birds within a flock can spend less time watching for predators and more time foraging—a major advantage when it comes to survival and breeding. It's also possible that the

---

## Did You Know?

Pigments and surface structure give feathers their amazing range of colors. Pigments called melanins, for example, generally produce shades of black and brown, while carotenoids create bright red, yellow, and orange. Pure white feathers have no pigment at all. Pigments can mingle to produce other feather colors, too. Birds manufacture some pigments internally; they obtain others from the flowers, roots, seeds, and fruits that they eat.

The external structure of the feather is another factor affecting its color. Blue is produced entirely through structural effects. And it gets even more complicated: pigments and structural effects together can result in a color, for instance, yellow pigment combined with blue structural color produces green, one of the more complex feather colors. Iridescent sheens result when minuscule surface patterns on the feathers interfere with the absorption or reflection of light waves.

---

hectic, noisy flight of many ducks could confuse a prowling coyote or attacking eagle long enough for the entire flock to make its getaway. The duck's powerful flocking instinct is a definite plus for duck keepers; it facilitates the task of herding the birds from place to place.

Ducks living together establish a pecking order just as chickens do, with one duck at the top ruling the flock; one duck at the bottom of the hierarchy; and everybody else in between. During mating season, wild ducks usually form pairs, performing elaborate courtship rituals that culminate in nest building, egg laying, and incubation of the eggs by the female duck. Domesticated drakes have apparently had this pairing instinct bred out of them; they are more likely to mate indiscriminately with any females in the flock.

Downy ducklings are precocial, meaning that once they recover from the strenuous hatching process (usually within a day or so), they're up on their little webbed feet, ready to leave the nest and search for their own food. Compare these independent babes with the altricial young of some other birds, such as the robin, that emerge naked and helpless. It's a good thing ducklings are so self-sufficient, too: although mother ducks do form an attachment to their young that lasts for almost a month, they're not nearly as attentive and protective as mother geese are.

## DUCK ANCESTRY

There are thirteen species of perching duck and thirty-nine species of dabbling duck that can be found throughout the world. Domestic ducks, the kind you commonly see on our farms today, descend from two species only—the wild Muscovy and the common Mallard. The Muscovy's large size no doubt made it a natural choice for domestication as a meat bird. As for the Mallard, this species may have been singled out for domestication because it was common and because it easily adapted to living near humans.

An attentive mother Muscovy watches over her precocial ducklings. Unlike altricial birds such as the Robin, ducklings start exploring their world and feeding themselves within a few days of hatching.

## WILD MUSCOVY (*CAIRINA MOSCHATA*)

Tentatively classified as a perching duck, this large, strange long-tailed duck of the tropics is the ancestor of the domestic Muscovy. Characterized by black plumage with an iridescent sheen and flashy white wing patches, the species inhabits wooded wetland areas from the Rio Grande in southern Texas, through Mexico, and all the way down to Central and South America. The male has black and red facial skin around the beak and eyes, and both sexes possess powerful claws to help them perch in trees. These nonmigratory waterfowl congregate in pairs or small flocks and prefer to nest in tree cavities and boxes. Their eclectic diet includes aquatic and terrestrial plants, insects, crustaceans, small fish, and reptiles.

According to some sources, the Incas of Peru domesticated Muscovies centuries ago, keeping them as pest-controlling pets and suppliers of feathers, eggs, and meat. Spanish conquistadors took these hefty ducks back with them from Columbia to Spain during the 1500s; from there, Muscovies were eventually imported to Africa, Asia, Australia, and North America. Along the way, this bird acquired many names, including Barbary duck, Brazilian duck, Turkish duck, Pato, and Guinea duck.

## COMMON MALLARD (*ANAS PLATYRHYNCHOS*)

All other farm ducks descend from the wild Mallard, thought to have been domesticated in China about four thousand years ago. The Mallard is a common dabbling duck that breeds on and

*A dapper wild Mallard drake shows off his yellow bill, iridescent green head, white neck collar, and chestnut breast as he glides across a lake.*

around shallow wetlands throughout North America and other parts of the Northern Hemisphere. Chances are you've encountered these adaptable birds at a park, a zoo pond, or a farm field near your home.

Even neophyte duck watchers have little problem identifying this popular game species. Mallard males flaunt shimmering green heads, white collars, chestnut breasts, and orange legs and feet.

When they explode into flight, the drakes flash vivid blue wing bars, bordered with white and black, called speculums. The female duck, which also brandishes a speculum, has subtle penciled-brown plumage that helps camouflage her as she sits on her eggs.

Mallards dine on a wide variety of foods, including acorns, grass, duckweed, fruits, algae, tadpoles, frogs, tiny fish, leeches, mosquito larvae, and crayfish. The female usually makes a shallow nest in cloaking vegetation near the water, where she lays a clutch of seven to ten eggs.

## ARE DUCKS RIGHT FOR YOU?

Now that you've been properly introduced to the amazing duck, you probably feel it's high time you zipped off to the feed store and nabbed some powder-puff ducklings. Not so fast! While a small duck flock can be a terrific addition to the farm, these birds have some characteristics that can drive an unprepared farmer to distraction. Before deciding to keep ducks, consider the following:

## DUCKS ARE MESSY

There's a reason Martha Stewart raises chickens and not ducks. Ducks consume a lot of food and water, and it all has to go somewhere. To put it plainly, these fowl produce copious amounts of wet droppings that have a truly unpleasant odor. During molting periods, their feathers and down fly far and wide. Ducks also love to dabble messily in

## Pros and Cons of Duck Ownership

Our experts discuss the practicalities of duck farming.

### Ducks Need Water

"One disadvantage of having ducks is that they do need a steady water source. People have reported being able to manage them without adequate pools for bathing, but that's not something I condone. Water is vitally important to ducks (they are known as waterfowl for a reason!), as it helps them stay healthy and keeps their feathers in good condition. Ducks that are given steady access to fresh, clean water rarely suffer from external parasites."

—*Cat Dreiling*

### Dealing with Quacks

"The females of most duck breeds quack incessantly; if you keep a yard light on all night, they'll stay up all night and quack. I started out with various breeds: Indian Runners, Blue Swedish, Rouens, Pekins. I enjoyed them all but got tired of the constant loud quacking. Then someone gave me a mixed batch of ducklings, some of which made a pleasing sort of whistling sound instead of a quack. I was sold on Muscovies!"

—*Melissa Peteler*

### Be a Good Neighbor

"The primary drawback to raising almost any kind of poultry today is the increasing frequency of restrictive ordinances, even in small towns. Be a good neighbor by keeping your birds clean and quiet. Keep them inside their housing until a decent time of morning. Landscape around duck pens and runs. Good landscaping can hide the pens from view as well as reduce noise. Planting ornamentals around a pen can also dress up the area. Share your surplus eggs."

—*Lou Horton*

their food dishes (thus attracting rodents), in their water containers, and in the puddles around their swimming holes. Too many ducks occupying too small an area can bring stinky ruin down on your farm and negatively impact groundwater and wetlands. On the bright side, proper management can keep the mess to a minimum, and all that duck manure makes great fertilizer!

## DUCKS CAN BE NOISY

Some folks love the quacking of a flock of ducks because it reminds them of the country; others prefer that ducks be seen and not heard. If you or your neighbors are sensitive to quacking, you might want to steer clear of gabby Call, Pekin, or Mallard females. Drakes of all dabbling duck breeds are less talkative. Muscovies are completely quackless: the drakes make a hissing sound and the females emit soft whistles and squeaks unless they're upset about something, in which case they might squawk. You can also mute the cacophony somewhat with landscaping or a solid fence. We'll look further into how to choose the right ducks in chapter 2.

## DUCKS CAN DESTROY GARDENS

In their enthusiastic search for snails, slugs, and other creepy crawlies, patrolling ducks will uproot young plants—or stomp them flat with those big, flapping feet. Ducks also relish tender vegetation, some flowers, and berries, which can lead to conflicts with humans who want to harvest these crops. Again, management techniques can help, and we'll show you some of these in subsequent chapters.

## DUCKS CAN CARRY ZOONOTIC DISEASES

All farm animals are capable of carrying zoonotic diseases, animal diseases that can be transmitted to humans. Commonsense practices such as washing your hands and cooking meat and eggs thoroughly will help you and your family avoid contracting salmonellosis or other illnesses from your flock. It also helps if you make sure that your ducks stay in

*One of my Muscovies eyes a new planting, probably searching for slugs and bugs. The problem is, he'll probably root out the young plants in his enthusiasm. My best bet? Protect the flowers with a wire cage until they grow bigger.*

Ducklings raised with kindness and plenty of attention make friendly, fascinating, and responsive pets. (That being said, they should never be bought on a whim or given as a surprise present, for reasons we'll go into later.) Even people-shy older ducks can learn to overcome their fear of humans, especially when coaxed with treats. Duck lovers describe their pet ducks lying at their feet like dogs, tapping at the door for handouts, and following them faithfully around the farm. Some people keep ducks as house pets—you can even purchase diapers made especially for ducks. Although my tame Muscovies dislike being picked up, they seem to enjoy having their back feathers stroked and being scratched about the head, neck, and chin. Some

pet ducks like to play: one family I spoke to has a Rouen duck that chases tennis balls. Take that, Fido!

the peak of health by keeping their home as clean as possible, providing a proper diet, and paying attention to biosecurity issues such as quarantines and pest control.

## DUCKS NEED PROTECTION

Ducks may be super swimmers, super healthy, and super self-reliant, but they aren't indestructible. These typically unaggressive fowl, along with their eggs and vulnerable young, can succumb to a variety of hungry predators, from snapping turtles and bald eagles to raccoons and coyotes. Domestic dogs and cats will also kill ducks and ducklings. It's up to us to defend our fowl with secure fences, nighttime housing, and other protective measures, which we'll cover extensively in chapter 3.

## LOCAL LAWS MAY PROHIBIT DUCKS

Finally, don't forget to check your local zoning laws, even if you live in what appears to be a rural area. Some places may have limits on the number of ducks you can keep, while others may prohibit poultry altogether.

# CHAPTER TWO

# Choosing the Right Ducks

Picking out ducks for your farm seems an easy task, requiring little research. After all, the American Poultry Association (APA) recognizes only 19 domestic duck breeds in its Standard of Perfection; compare this with its recognition of 113 chicken breeds or with the American Kennel Club's listing of 145 dog breeds. Granted, an uninformed duck buyer won't get into nearly as much trouble as someone who acquires, say, a St. Bernard without doing any homework! Nevertheless, ducks do differ, and taking time to do some research into duck breed diversity can save the prospective duck farmer some frustration.

As mentioned in chapter 1, with the exception of the Muscovy, domestic duck breeds descend from the ubiquitous wild Mallard. Through the years, selective breeding by fanciers and farmers has produced a number of Mallard-derivative breeds in a charming mix of colors, shapes, and sizes. Like dog or chicken breeds, each recognized duck breed has certain desirable characteristics, from plumage color to egg output, that distinguish it from other breeds. For example, a big white Pekin duck looks very different from a skinny Runner duck, and the two differ considerably in their egg-laying prowess. They don't even act the same—in general, the Pekin has a more laid-back personality than does the active, true-to-its-name Runner.

Don't expect all individuals of a certain duck breed to be clones of one another, however. Some duck breeds are divided into varieties, usually denoted by plumage color or pattern. Call ducks, for instance, have many colorful types, including Buff, Snowy, Pastel, and White. Various strains—birds descended from one flock or breeding farm—exist as well. Breeding and environmental factors such as diet or

*The Snowy Call duck pictured here is just one of a number of delightful color varieties developed by breeders over the years.*

imprinting (a rapid learning process by which a duckling learns to recognize and become attracted to another duck, animal, or object) can also produce variations in size, color, personality, and more.

## MEET THE BREEDS

Now let's meet a few of the more commonly raised duck breeds from each of the four APA classes: bantam, lightweight, middleweight, and heavyweight. But don't limit yourself to these ducks—see the box "Keeping Endangered Duck Breeds" to find out about the endangered birds listed by the American Livestock Breeds Conservancy (ALBC). Other duck types have developed in various parts of the United States as well as in other countries, and certainly more will appear in years to come. So keep your eyes open—you may stumble upon an interesting breed, such as the Dutch Hookbill or Silky Bantam, that is not listed by either the APA or the ALBC.

## BANTAMS: LITTLE DUCKS, BIG PERSONALITIES

It seems that nearly every type of livestock has been subject to selective breeding to create miniature breeds perfect for smaller spaces. Bantam ducks, weighing in at a slim one to three pounds, make easy-to-handle exhibition fowl, friendly and amusing pets, and even tasty meat birds. Their small size doesn't keep them from consuming their fair share of bugs and slugs, and it enables them to fly really well. Another plus: they eat smaller amounts of concentrated feed than their big brothers and sisters do. Their size is influenced by genetics, environment, and nutrition, so if you plan to raise and breed bantams, you'll have to pay attention to proper selection and management to keep them small. The APA recognizes four bantam breeds: the Mallard, the Call, the East Indies, and the Australian Spotted (the

*A White Call duck fits neatly into the keeper's hand. Classified as a Bantam duck, Calls are popular for exhibition—plus they're friendly and oh so cute. Bantam breeds generally weigh three pounds or less.*

As you're mulling over the various duck breeds, ask yourself the following:

*How much space do you have for ducks?* The APA classifies ducks by size from bantam (the smallest) to heavy-weight (the largest). Cute bantam ducks such as the Call or the Australian Spotted usually require less space than big ducks do. These petite waterfowl are talented fliers, though, meaning they may be less likely to stay close to home unless wing-clipped or penned.

*What do you want from your ducks?* Baskets of eggs, meat for the table, slug and snail control, blue ribbons, adornment for your farm, or feathered friendship? For example, you'll get plenty of eggs from a Campbell but not a whole lot of meat, whereas in the White Aylesbury, you'll have a meaty bird, but one that lays compara-tively few eggs. Some breeds, such as the medium-size Orpington, have been bred as all-purpose ducks: these fowl lay a fair number of eggs and yield a decent meat carcass.

*What kind of housing and predator protection can you provide?* Slow-waddling and meek, the grounded Pekin is more vulnerable to predators than is the feisty, flighted Muscovy. The Muscovy, however, with its bare face and tropical ancestry, can't cope with freezing weather as well as the Pekin can.

*How do you plan to feed and house your ducks?* Will you keep your ducks in pens and serve them bagged chow or let them roam around your orchard and pastures hunting for their own vittles? The heavy breeds, with the exception of the Muscovy, don't forage as much as the lighter breeds do. The energetic Runner, bred to dash about gobbling up pests and other natural foods, won't adapt to pen confinement as well as the slower Rouen will.

*Do you plan to breed ducks?* Some breeds, such as the Muscovy and ban-tam ducks, will enthusiastically incubate their own eggs and raise ducklings. Other breeds couldn't care less, which means you'll need either broody fowl (birds eager to incubate eggs) or an incubator to do the job. If you set out to breed Muscovies, you'll quickly discover that Muscovy females excel at hiding their nests. Without a population con-trol or marketing plan in place, you could find yourself drowning in ducks!

*Do you have small children?* Ducks, for the most part, are gentle birds, but some Muscovy drakes can be nearly as aggressive as a cranky goose. Their powerful legs and sharp claws also make them a challenge for even an adult to handle.

first three breeds are described below; read about the Australian Spotted in appendix A, "Endangered Duck Breeds").

## The Mallard

Domestic Mallard drakes look just as flashy as their wild counterparts do, with vivid green heads, white neck rings, yellow bills, and chestnut breasts. Females have inconspicuous but lovely streaked brown coloring that comes in handy as camouflage when they incubate their buff, green, or bluish eggs. The ducklings sport yellow down with black markings. Domestic Mallards, weighing in at two and a half to three pounds, while different from their slender wild kin in size, are similar in their ability to brood their eggs and forage well. Keepers often raise Mallards for meat, for show, for hunting, and as decorative additions to the farm. Some states may require a permit to raise and sell these birds, so be sure to check first. Varieties include Gray (the wild coloration), White, and Golden.

These Saxony Call ducks look like round-headed Mallards in miniature.

## The Call Duck

Except for their fuzzy young, ducks don't get any cuter than the compact Call duck, with its plump body, round head, and stubby beak and legs. Weighing less than two pounds, these birds come in an engaging variety of colors and patterns, including pure white and magpie. The Gray Call looks similar to the wild Mallard.

Calls make friendly pets and beautiful exhibition birds and, like other bantams, require less living space and food than the bigger birds do. Females lay sixty to seventy-five eggs a year and tend to be reliable setters and mothers. The ducklings are described as delicate. Be advised that Calls are the toddlers of the duck world: active and noisy! The breed's name derives from the ducks' shrill, carrying vocalizations, which hunters historically exploited to lure wild ducks into traps or within shooting range. Federal law banned the use of live decoys in 1934.

Domestic Mallards of the gray variety look similar to their wild kin, pictured here dabbling on a sunny lake. They're excellent brooders and foragers.

# Keeping Endangered Duck Breeds

If you've decided to add ducks to your farm, consider raising an endangered breed. Agricultural industrialization, fueled by an obsession with maximum profit and efficiency, has led to the livestock industry's being dominated by a few breeds and hybrids, while other unique breeds have declined alarmingly or vanished altogether. Rare breeds—rare because fewer farmers keep and breed them—tend to be hardier than their commercial counterparts and better at foraging. They're beautiful, often important historically, and possess genotypic variations that could become important for agriculture down the road.

The American Livestock Breed Conservancy (ALBC), a nonprofit organization based in Pittsboro, North Carolina, has worked since 1977 to conserve and maintain the genetic diversity of nearly 100 breeds of horses, cattle, asses, sheep, goats, pigs, and poultry. The organization's work embraces education, conservation, and research programs, including a periodic census of livestock breeds and the publication of conservation priority lists.

For more information on which ducks breeds are under threat, see appendix A, "Endangered Duck Breeds." Then check out the resource list for hatcheries and breeders that offer these rarer fowl.

## The East Indies Duck

This exquisite breed looks as exotic as its name. Dressed in inky black plumage with a shimmering green iridescence, this breed is also known as the Emerald, Brazilian, or Labrador duck. It is thought to have been developed over a span of about 200 years, from the early 1800s to the late 1900s, in North America and Britain.

Too gorgeous and petite to raise for meat production, these ducks are popular for show or decoration and as pets. Somewhat quieter than Calls, the females make good setters and mothers. East Indies produce up to seventy-five eggs a year—dark gray-green eggs

*A handsome East Indies duck flaunts the shimmering iridescence that makes these bantam birds popular as pets and show fowl.*

# Duck Matchmaker

| You're looking for | Breeds to think about |
| --- | --- |
| A prolific egg producer | Campbell, Harlequin, Magpie, Runner, Ancona, Orpington, Appleyard, Saxony |
| A hefty meat duck | Muscovy, Rouen, Aylesbury, Pekin, Saxony, Appleyard |
| A good sitter and mother | Bantam breeds, Muscovy |
| A quieter duck than most | Muscovy, drakes of the dabbler breeds |

at the start of the season, then progressively paler eggs as the laying season draws to a close.

## LIGHTWEIGHTS: THE SUPER LAYERS

If you want a super egg-laying duck that's unlikely to go broody on you and try to incubate every egg that's laid, then take a gander at one of the lightweight breeds. At three and a half pounds to a bit over five pounds, these active birds tend to be enthusiastic snail and slug foragers, only so-so flyers, and a bit more land loving than other breeds. The APA recognizes the following lightweights: Runner, Campbell, Welsh Harlequin, and Magpie. The Runner and the Campbell are described below; read about the Welsh Harlequin and the Magpie in appendix A, "Endangered Duck Breeds."

## The Runner

The aptly named Runner duck descended from fowl traditionally herded between home and rice paddy in parts of Asia. The movie *Babe,* about a sheepherding pig, featured a Runner duck in its supporting cast—not surprising, given this duck's active personality and amusing looks. Weighing around four pounds, Runner ducks have a skinny, upright body resembling a bowling pin on legs that enables them to cover ground fast. Their eggs are white, and they can pump out up to 300 of them a year—just don't ask them to sit on the eggs! The Bali, one of the oldest breeds of domestic duck, looks like the Runner except for the rounded crest on its head.

Runners come in a wide variety of colors and patterns, including chocolate, buff, black, gray, fawn, and fawn and white. They make fun, pest-consuming pets and popular exhibition fowl.

## The Campbell

An egg-layer extraordinaire, this breed owes its existence to Ms. Adele Campbell of England, who produced the Mallard-like breed from Runner, Rouen, and Mallard stock in the late 1800s. She eventually selected for an attractive, tan-colored bird that resembled the khaki uniforms of British soldiers. The Khaki Campbell is still the most popular type, although white and pied varieties also exist.

Campbells that are selected for high egg production rank as the most prolific layers of all the duck breeds; they produce white eggs and can lay up to 350 a year. They're also hardy birds that can adapt to a wide range of environments and climates.

## MIDDLEWEIGHTS: THE DO-IT-ALL DUCKS

Weighing in at around six to eight pounds, these all-purpose ducks fall between the light and heavy classes in terms of size, laying ability, growth rate, and meat yield. They make good pest-gobbling foragers and are generally calm pets. Middleweights recognized by the APA are the Cayuga, the Crested, the Ancona, the Orpington, and the Swedish breeds (read about Ancona, Orpington, and Swedish ducks in appendix A, "Endangered Duck Breeds"). If you want a good all-purpose fowl that does a bit of everything, these birds deserve a look.

## The Cayuga

Developed in New York during the early 1800s and named for Lake Cayuga, the Cayuga ranks as one of the most beautiful of the domestic ducks. In the traditional black variety, its pitch-dark plumage glows with an iridescent green sheen, accented by a blue wing speculum. In a year, females lay more than 100 eggs, ranging in color from dark gray to green to white during the season. Although not very many Cayuga are being bred, they are frequent competitors at poultry shows.

*Middleweight duck breeds, such as this stunning Cayuga drake, are good all-purpose farm ducks that weigh around six to eight pounds. The Cayuga breed hails from New York, and females can lay more than 100 eggs a year.*

## The Crested Duck

Another easily identifiable breed is the Crested duck. The APA recognizes two varieties of this breed: the black and the white. The latter looks like a Pekin with a fancy feathered headdress. The eye-catching crest, caused by a dominant mutation, has made these ducks popular as unusual pets and pond ornaments; they also provide a good supply of eggs—100 or more a year. According to

*A Crested duck of the white variety takes a waddle. The Crested duck's fancy topknot is the result of a dominant mutation and has made this middleweight breed popular among duck enthusiasts.*

waterfowl raiser Dave Holderread, breeding for crests can be challenging because of health problems, such as premature embryo death and skeletal abnormalities, sometimes associated with this mutation.

## HEAVYWEIGHTS: THE MIGHTY DUCKS

Heavyweights such as the Pekin and Muscovy (described below) and the rarer Appleyard, Aylesbury, Rouen, and Saxony (listed in appendix A, "Endangered Duck Breeds") weigh seven to fifteen pounds. This makes them the first choice for farmers who want to raise ducks primarily for meat production. These big birds also make placid pets, and they usually stay close to home because the weight of their hefty bodies makes flying difficult. Two exceptions are female and younger male Muscovies, whose powerful wings help them take flight with ease. Heavyweight ducks grow like weeds. This is great if you're raising them for meat, but if you plan to keep them long term as breeders or feathered companions, you'll need to take steps to prevent overly rapid growth, which can lead to leg deformities and lameness.

## The Pekin

Chances are good you've tossed bread to snowy Pekin ducks on a pond somewhere or savored this duck's rich and succulent meat at an Asian restaurant. Probably the best known and most common domestic duck breed, the Pekin traces its history back to ancient China. The first Pekins in the United States arrived in New York City from Peking (now Beijing), China, back in 1873.

Mellow and hardy, Pekins pack on the pounds at lightning speed, making them the commercial duck of choice for meat production purposes. Reaching nine to ten pounds, these birds efficiently convert forage and feed to muscle and also produce a fair number of whitish eggs each year (around 100 to 175). However, they tend to be poor sitters and mothers.

Pekins are easy to identify: their plumage is white, often with a creamy cast, and they have wide bodies, thick necks, and orange bills and feet. Pekin babies—think of the stereotypical Easter

*"Pekins rule!" this bathing beauty seems to say. It's no wonder Pekin ducks adorn so many farm (and park) ponds: these mellow, hardy birds grow fast, efficiently converting feed to tasty meat, and they produce a decent number of eggs as well.*

duckling—have cheerful yellow down, and they imprint easily on the people who raise them, becoming incredibly tame. Pekins make friendly, amusing pets and look lovely parading across a green pasture or lawn.

## The Muscovy

Domestic Muscovies waddle to the beat of a different drummer than the Mallard-derivative dabblers do. In fact, Muscovies, adapted for perching in trees, don't really fit the duck image. For one, they aren't nearly as crazy about water as dabblers are. As mentioned, they're also quackless; the males make a quiet hissing sound, while the females emit breathy squeaks (although they will squawk if frightened).

*One of the heavyweight meat breeds, this beautiful Saxony drake has a hefty body that prevents him from flying the coop. The big ducks also make dandy pets, but you'll need to put the breaks on their rapid growth with careful feeding to prevent leg problems.*

Muscovies are big, strapping ducks, great for meat production, with males weighing up to fifteen pounds and females averaging eight pounds. Their meat contains less fat than that of dabbling ducks. Despite their large size, females and young males are powerful fliers, and both sexes possess sharp claws that enable them to perch in trees and on barns (or even on your house roof).

Muscovies are good foragers. They love slugs and worms, among other garden delicacies. The females take first prize as outstanding setters and marvelously protective mothers. They don't produce a lot of eggs throughout the year, but they do set several clutches of up to twenty waxy, cream-colored eggs for an incubation period of about thirty-five days. Muscovy drakes have unforgettable faces. The beaks and eyes are surrounded by brilliant red skin adorned with fleshy, wartlike growths called caruncles. The females have only a bit of bare skin on their faces. The APA recognizes four colors—black (the wild coloration), blue, white, and chocolate. Fanciers have selected for other colors as well, such as lavender, calical, blue and white, and chocolate and white.

## SELECTING YOUR FIRST DUCKS

Once you've settled on a duck breed (or two or three), you'll need to make a few more decisions before you have the pleasure of watching your own flock waddle about your farm.

### EGGS, DUCKLINGS, OR ADULTS?

You can purchase hatching eggs, ducklings, or adult birds to start your flock. Each option has its pros and cons. Hatching eggs—fertile eggs that have been carefully selected and handled—may cost slightly less than ducklings, but they could be damaged during transit, and there's no guarantee that every egg will hatch. You'll also need an artificial incubator or a broody bird (either a hen or a duck that will sit on eggs) to incubate them.

*My Muscovy drake, Dandy Duck, surveys his domain. Dandy exhibits the characteristic bright red skin and facial caruncles of all Muscovy drakes.*

# Love at First Quack

Years ago, I met my first Muscovy duck while working at the San Antonio Zoo as a bird keeper. A dedicated broody bird, always eager to sit on eggs, Ms. Muscovy had been drafted by zoo staff to incubate a swan egg. Because she couldn't turn such a large egg by herself (see chapter 5 on egg turning), it was my duty to visit her nest three times a day and turn the egg. I expected this rather large duck to put up a fuss when I reached under her for the first time—and maybe even bite me—but she didn't. On subsequent visits, I talked to her and stroked her sleek white feathers, admiring her patience, and she conversed back in breathy, friendly whistles. In some weird, maternal way, we bonded over that egg. I can't remember if Ms. Muscovy ever hatched her swan egg, but I'll never forget that duck. Muscovies have been my favorite fowl ever since.

Ducklings are adorable and fun to raise, and they do surprisingly well when properly shipped from commercial hatcheries, each duckling traveling complete with its own food supply in the form of its yolk sac. Yet, ducklings require more specialized care (and thus, more of your time) than mature ducks do. It also takes a while before they produce eggs and meat, breed, or embark on pest and pond plant control.

Purchasing adult ducks may seem like a good way to go, but depending on the ducks' age—and that could be a big question mark if the breeder hasn't kept good records—they might not have as long a productive life ahead of them as youngsters would. It may also take some time for them to get used to your farm, and temporary wing clipping might be required for flighted breeds to keep them home at first. If you do choose grown ducks, you will need to have their outside abode prepared (see chapter 3) before they arrive on the farm.

*To start your duck flock, you can order hatching eggs like these. Hatching eggs are fertile duck eggs that have been carefully selected and handled to increase hatching success, but that doesn't guarantee they will all hatch.*

## Wild Ornamentals

One other delightful group of ducks deserves mention, although we won't be focusing on them in this book. These are the ornamentals: wild duck species from around the world kept not for meat or eggs or bug control but simply because they captivate waterfowl lovers with their beautiful plumage and interesting behaviors. Species include the exotic Mandarin, the showy North American Wood duck, the vivid Cinnamon Teal, and the little Ringed Teal from South America.

Caring for wild waterfowl is in many ways similar to caring for domestic duck breeds, but there are some notable differences. For instance, ornamentals generally require more space, especially if you want to breed them. Unlike most domestic duck breeds, they also excel at flying; covered enclosures or wing clipping may be required to keep them from taking off. Before you get involved with these stunning creatures, study up on the different species and their care requirements. You need a permit to keep native wildfowl such as the Ruddy duck and Pintail, so contact your state Department of Natural Resources first.

## MALES, FEMALES, OR BOTH?

Although there's no way of knowing which sex duckling will pop out of a hatching egg, you can buy ducklings that are already sexed from a hatchery for a slightly higher price. By the way, if you buy them unsexed, you can expect that the sexes will be evenly split—at least, that's the theory. Waterfowl are one of the few bird species in which the male possesses a penis, so a duckling can be vent-sexed by inverting the cloaca to see if a penis is present. This procedure, however, requires a gentle, practiced hand to avoid injuring the duckling. Do not attempt it without the guidance of an expert.

Fortunately, the sex of mature males and females is fairly easy to determine without an internal exam. In the case of Muscovies, males grow much larger and have more caruncles on their faces than females do. Dabbler drakes often have gaudier plumage than the ducks have—the Mallard is a good example. In breeds with similar sexes, such as White Runners or Aylesbury ducks, the drake has curled "sex" feathers above his tail.

Whether you should get drakes, ducks, or both depends on a few factors. If you want to produce ducklings, obviously you need both sexes. Some raisers keep their breeder birds in pairs for the breeding season, while others use varying ratios (one drake to multiple females). If you want the ducks as pets, all females or all males will be fine except in the case of the territorial, often aggressive Muscovy drakes. If it's egg production you're after, all females will do. Like chickens, ducks will lay eggs without a drake on the premises. The eggs will be infertile, but that's fine if you just want to eat them and not breed more ducks.

## How Many Ducks?

Ducks are social creatures, so unless you plan to be an only duck's best friend and can give it ample attention, you'll want your bird to have some feathered companions. If you order hatching eggs or ducklings from a hatchery, you generally have to buy in bulk. McMurray Hatchery in Iowa, for instance, has a minimum shipping order of ten ducklings to ensure that the babies stay warm in transit.

Before you order, take a look at your farm and water sources. Too large a flock crammed in too small an area and bathing in one tiny pond will make an odorous, unhealthy mess. (For more information on housing your flock, see

*To tell the difference between similar-looking adult male and female ducks of the dabbler breeds, look for the male's curled sex feather, proudly displayed by this preening white Magpie drake.*

# Advice from the Farm

## Choosing Duck Breeds

Our experts weigh in with advice on finding the best fit for you.

### Know the Breeds

"Everyone will have a breed of duck that 'fits' their situation better than another. While the Muscovy is a wonderful duck to have on my farm, it does have some characteristics that aren't pleasant. Muscovies are omnivorous and will eat a number of small creatures, be it a frog or a baby bird. They'll also eat chicks and other ducklings, something that can be quite traumatic to experience. They're incredibly strong, and it's tough to handle them at times due to their physical strength and talonlike claws. I think if individuals learn all they can about the characteristics of the different duck breeds prior to buying, they'll save a lot of time and hassle in the long run than if they just picked a few ducklings from a bin at the farm supply store."

*—Cat Dreiling*

### Prepurchase Questions

"What are your rearing facilities like? Big duck breeds require much more space per bird. They also eat more than light and bantam breeds do. Calls, East Indies, Mallards, and Mandarins can fly. How will you design your pens or manage your flock to accommodate that quality? Decide before you purchase your ducks what you'll primarily want to keep them for. For show? Consider Calls, East Indies, Cayuga, and Runners (especially Whites). Birds for both meat and eggs: Khaki Campbells, Buff Orpingtons, and Magpie ducks. For meat, there's no bird superior to the Muscovy, and it's hard to beat Runners and Campbells for eggs."

*—Lou Horton*

### Breed Differences

"We tried Muscovies, but they were too aggressive—they tried to kill the other ducks' babies. Now we keep Indian Runners, Khaki Campbells, and Blue Swedish.

They're all good slug eaters, and the Campbells and Runners lay a lot of eggs, which we like. The Runners are good foragers, but they're indifferent mothers; they don't seem to

have the patience to hatch out their ducklings. They're also highly excitable. The Khaki Campbells are calmer. The Blue Swedish are friendly, and they lay fairly well; they're determined to be mothers."

—*Angie Pilch*

### Multipurpose Muscovies

"Not only are Muscovies quiet, but they're very large meat birds and often able to defend themselves (although I once lost a full-grown duck to a bald eagle). The ducks make excellent mothers—all my ducklings are raised by their mothers—and our little flock keeps our yard relatively free of grasshoppers in the summer."

— *Melissa Peteler*

### Popular Pekins

"I really enjoy Pekins. I don't like to use poisonous slug bait, and Pekins are great for slug control. They take care of all my flower beds, plus they don't dig up the beds the way chickens do. Unfortunately, these ducks grow fast and can have leg problems as a result (we've only had one experience with leg problems in a Pekin). All of our Pekins have been very mellow and friendly, with the exception of one attack drake that made a great guard duck—he wouldn't let any dogs or people near his girlfriend."

— *Trish Smith*

*As social animals, ducks such as these Aylesburies and Golden Cascades love the security and stimulation of living in a flock. You should avoid keeping just one duck alone.*

chapter 3.) Although you don't want to begin with more ducks than you can manage, you also should avoid starting out with too few; adding birds later can upset the pecking order and also risks introducing disease or parasites. Keep in mind that some fluctuation in flock numbers is to be expected: breeding—both planned and unplanned—will add to the flock; at the same time, predators, accidents, illness, and culling will take their toll. Whatever your purpose for keeping ducks, your best bet is to start with a small flock of two to ten birds until you've learned the ropes of duck keeping.

## WHEN YOU'RE READY TO BUY

Finding ducks isn't difficult: in spring, you'll see Easter ducklings on sale at your local feed store or ads for surplus ducks in the newspapers. Finding the ducks you want—healthy, of good show stock, the right breed, and so on—can be more challenging. For hatching eggs, day-old ducklings, and sometimes adult ducks, check out reputable hatcheries and breeders (see the Resources section). You can also purchase ducklings of more common breeds at feed stores and obtain ducklings and mature stock from local farmers. If you are able to be there in person to pick out your ducks, look for active, healthy birds with bright eyes, clean vents, and strong legs. Use special care when picking out ducks for breeding stock.

Most duck raisers start their flocks in the spring or summer, when feed stores carry ducklings and breeders have extra stock to sell. Depending on the hatchery, you may be able to order ducklings and hatching eggs from spring through fall.

In the next chapter, we'll look at where your ducks will be sleeping, waddling, swimming, and eating when they take up residence on your farm.

# CHAPTER THREE

# Housing Your Flock

W ell protected within their insulating waterproof plumage and down, domestic ducks have adapted to a range of climates around the world. You'll find them weathering midwestern snows and southwestern heat waves in the United States, heavy downpours in the British Isles, and stifling humidity in Central American rain forests. When other wimpy livestock race to the barn during a rain shower, ducks stay outside and revel in it. While chickens remain tucked in their cozy coops on a snowy winter day, ducks dabble blithely about their ice-rimmed pond. Mature ducks typically don't require the sort of snug accommodations many folks fashion for their chickens, especially in areas with fairly mild winters. Like wild waterfowl, most domestic dabblers would be content to spend their nights sheltering beneath a bush or floating on a pond. Flighted Muscovies often prefer taking to the trees or some other lofty perch.

Many small flock raisers, however, do provide their ducks with indoor housing or a covered shelter—and not just because they feel like spoiling their feathered friends. Giving ducks a refuge from weather extremes improves egg and meat production; after all, it takes energy for ducks to keep themselves warm or cool themselves off, energy they could use laying eggs and putting on pounds. Not only that, but when exposed to frigid weather, ducks—especially the cold-sensitive Muscovy—risk frostbite to their feet.

Along with providing a house or shelter for their ducks, many raisers keep their birds partially or completely confined in outdoor duck yards, pens, or fenced pastures. An enclosure of some type comes in handy for preventing these ever-foraging fowl from rooting up your spring veggie starts, sleeping—and messing—on your deck, or wandering out onto the road and over to your neighbor's garden.

Secure housing and pens serve an even more important purpose: protection from the host of varmints that will dine on duck eggs, ducklings, or adult ducks if given an easy opportunity to do so. Most domestic ducks, with the possible exception of some fierce, flying Muscovies, truly are "sitting ducks." As a rule, ducks tend to be noisy, colorful, unaggressive, slow on land, and incapable of swift flight (if they can fly at all)—all traits that make them attractive to wild and domestic predators.

## HOUSING BASICS

Along with adapting easily to various climates, ducks adjust well to many different housing arrangements. You don't have to spend a bundle to provide them with adequate shelter. Keepers of small duck flocks successfully use a variety of accommodations for their fowl, from simple Igloo doghouses, revamped chicken coops, livestock stalls, and dog kennels to beautiful custom-made wood abodes and netted aviaries designed especially for ornamental ducks. How large or elaborate your ducks' home should be depends on a number of factors, including your climate,

*Housing for your flock doesn't have to be expensive or elaborate. This accommodation provides everything a duck needs in a home: safety from predators, shelter from the elements, swimming and drinking water, a dining area, and a clean environment. Oh—and plenty of room to act like a duck.*

# Housing Options

| Keep in mind | Here's why |
|---|---|
| The size of your flock | A doghouse or plastic dog crate might suffice for a pet Pekin or two, but a flock of six will need more spacious quarters. |
| Which breeds you plan to keep | You'll need a bigger house for a pair of fat Rouen ducks than for a pair of petite Call ducks. |
| How many breeds you plan to raise | Different breeds will require separate pens during breeding season, or you may end up with hybrids. |
| The requirements for egg or meat production | Layers kept for a number of years need more permanent housing than rapidly growing, short-lived meat birds do. |
| How much of the time your ducks will be confined (night and day, part of the time, or not at all) | Confined ducks need more lodging room than do birds allowed to roam free. |
| The predators that frequent the area | If owls or eagles pay regular visits, overhead netting on pens may be critical. If raccoons live in the area, you'll need a varmint-proof house you can tuck your ducks into every night: raccoons scale fences with ease. |

finances, time constraints, local building regulations, and more.

Here are some points to consider when planning a refuge for your ducks:

## HOUSING SPECIFICS

Before you draw up plans for a duck house and yard or modify an existing structure, keep in mind the following important guidelines.

## SPACE REQUIREMENTS

One of the joys of keeping your own small flock of ducks is knowing that your birds have more space to engage in natural behaviors such as preening, bathing, and foraging than do birds kept on commercial farms. Ducks crowded tightly together in houses experience stress that can lead to feather picking, and they can overheat on hot days. At

*Crowding can increase stress and promote disease, so plan to give your ducks as much room as possible when constructing houses and pens. The enclosures shown here give birds enough space to bathe, preen, and stretch their legs.*

the very minimum, a house for mature ducks that have access to an outdoor pen or pasture should allow two to four square feet per bird, depending on the breed's size. So for a flock of ten ducks, you will need a house or shelter of approximately twenty to forty square feet. (This does not include storage space for supplies, which are best housed in a separate shed.) Birds confined full time need at least twice that much space—more, if possible. Remember, too, that doors for ducks to pass through must be wide enough that the birds won't trample one another when moving in and out of the house.

If you don't clean your duck enclosure daily, manure and filth will build up. This accumulation is not only unsightly and smelly but also unhealthy for your birds, as it increases the risk of parasite and disease transmission. So when planning outer yards, remember that larger, less packed pens will stay cleaner longer than small, overpopulated ones. If you rotate yards or use portable pens that can be moved from place to place, you can probably get by with less roomy digs for your ducks.

## WHERE TO PLACE THE SHELTER

Avoid placing your ducks' new abode in a low spot or smack up against your neighbor's property. Take into account, too, how far away you plan to store your cleaning supplies and feed and where the nearest electrical outlet and water spigot are. A slightly sloped site with well-draining sandy or gravelly soil is ideal. Take advantage of existing trees or shrubs, using them as wind breaks, as sound and visual barriers, or for shade. Plant more trees and shrubs if necessary; ducks require protection from wind-lashed snow and rain as well as from hot summer sun.

Think about how you want to access the house and yard for cleaning, feeding, gathering eggs, and watering; easy access will save you much time and frustration. If you plan to keep flighted ornamental waterfowl in an aviary setting, consider doing what many zoos do: establish a safety area—a covered area that has its own entrance and exit door—adjoining the aviary. This allows you to go in and out of the aviary but prevents any birds from escaping.

## How to Ventilate

Ducks need to breathe oxygen, just as other animals do. Air quality can suffer in a tightly closed house, where ammonia fumes rise from manure and dust accumulates from feed and litter, adding to the feather dust and carbon dioxide given off by the ducks themselves. These pollutants can adversely affect a duck's eyes and respiratory tract—and yours, too, if you're working inside the duck house. Windows or slatted vents, located at the top of the building to prevent ground-level drafts, will not only add ventilation but also help eliminate mold-promoting moisture in your duck house. Cover any windows or other ventilation

*A slightly sloped site such as this one makes for good drainage—and that means less mud in your ducks' yard or pen.*

openings with sturdy, well-attached screen or wire to prevent predators from sneaking into the house.

## WEATHERPROOFING

The duck house or shelter should have a decent roof to shield against rain and snow. Even water-loving waterfowl enjoy an opportunity to dry off now and then. If you live in an area with mild winters and summers, your duck house can probably do without insulation. But if sweltering summers or freezing winters are the norm, give your ducks access to an insulated house that keeps temperatures steady, and you'll find that they consume less feed and produce more eggs and meat.

Adult ducks don't normally need artificial heating in their houses, especially if they have buddies to huddle up

*A Pekin finds cooling shade under a tree. Trees and shrubs make excellent natural sunshades in duck pens and pastures.*

to during cold weather (ducklings are a different story—see chapter 5). In a pinch, you can pile bales of straw or hay around the house for insulation. During hot weather, you may need to set up a sprinkler or misting system if your birds show signs of heat stress, such as panting. If you keep your ducks in outside yards and pastures, remember to provide them with shade, either natural or constructed, so that they can escape the sun. Trees, shrubs, wood shelters, and tarps can also double as shelters from rain and from snow.

## FLOORING, LITTER, AND SUBSTRATE

Duck house floors commonly consist of cement, packed dirt, or wood. Cement, though probably the costliest option, works well for keeping rodents and other predators from tunneling into the house. A cement floor is simple to clean with a hose and scrub brush, provided it is properly graded to prevent puddle-forming dips. Cover the cement with a soft layer of litter to soak up the moisture in the ducks' droppings (droppings are about 90 percent water). The litter will also protect your ducks' feet, which are smoother and more sensitive than tough chicken feet and easily get abrasions from a hard surface. Dirt and wooden floors also require bedding to absorb moisture. A cushiony litter will help your birds stay warm during winter, too.

Litter should consist of a clean, dry, absorbent material such as nontoxic pine shavings, quality hardwood chips

The cushy layer of litter in this duck house protects the occupants' sensitive feet from abrasions, soaks up wet droppings and spilled water, and provides a soft surface for laying eggs. It will also help keep the flock warm when winter comes.

(other than walnut, which is potentially toxic), crushed corn cobs, and rice hulls. Many farmers use straw, but it's less absorbent than other materials. Look for these materials at your local feed store. Steer clear of grass or legume hays for bedding; these can quickly turn moldy.

Some raisers keep ducks in wire-floored cages, particularly for exhibition. Again, because ducks' feet and legs are susceptible to injury, make sure that the wire you use has no sharp edges and that the mesh size is no larger than one inch by half an inch in size. Sprinkling litter in part of the cage will give the birds a comfortable place to sit if the wire hurts their feet.

Outer pens and yards located on bare soil with poor drainage often require an added substrate to keep the ducks from trampling and dabbling the ground to mud. Mud not only makes for unsightly lodgings and dirty plumage but also teems with bacteria and fungal organisms, some of which can cause health problems. During wet weather, the nutrients, sediments, and bacteria from mud and droppings run off into surface and ground waters, polluting wetlands and drinking water. Good substrate materials include sand, pea gravel, straw, sawdust, and a combination of these materials.

## FEEDERS AND WATERERS

When outfitting your duck digs with feeders and waterers, choose containers that are durable, easy to clean, and stable enough that the ducks can't flip them over in their enthusiasm to get to the food or water. Feed stores and livestock or poultry supply companies carry a plethora of poultry feeders and waterers to choose from. You'll also find round, shallow pans for general livestock use; they are made of rubber or hard plastic and make long-lasting, stable water con-

Here, a hanging metal feeder serves as a dining table for ducks. It is durable, won't tip, and is easy to clean, and there's room for everyone to eat—in a word, perfect!

tainers and feed dishes. Check out thrift stores and yard sales for tough stainless steel pans and bowls if you want to save money. Ducks aren't picky.

While almost anything that works for chickens will suffice for ducks, remember that waterfowl have larger, broader bills than pointy-beaked chickens do, so make sure the feeder and waterer you choose have wide enough troughs. Allow plenty of feeder space so all of your ducks, high- and low-ranking alike, can eat at the same time. Water containers for ducks should be at least three inches deep so the birds can submerge their heads to keep their eyes and nostrils clean and healthy. To help keep litter dry in the duck house, consider placing waterers in an outer yard. If your ducks spend the night in the house and have food available to them, however, they'll also need water to prevent them from choking on the feed. You can

avoid some of the inevitable mess by setting the containers on mesh or on wooden slats.

## NEST SITES

Although domestic dabbling ducks have a tendency to drop their eggs anywhere, some will make nests on the ground. To increase your chances of getting clean eggs, set up nest boxes at ground level along the sides of the house or pen, and bed them with shavings or straw. You can even build a nest box area into the duck house itself (of course, there's no guarantee your ducks will opt to use the nest boxes). Provide at least one twelve-by-twelve-inch (or larger, if needed) nest box for every four birds. If building a box from wood, leave one end open and nail a two- to three-inch strip of wood along the bottom edge of the open end. This will help keep the nesting material and eggs inside the box. Plastic dog ken-

*This pair of Pekins have a nice deep water tub that allows them to submerge their heads completely, thus keeping their nostrils, eyes, and mouths clean and healthy.*

*Ducks are messy creatures, and that's a fact: setting the birds' water pans atop wire mesh, as shown above, will help keep the mess down.*

nels with the doors removed, covered kitty litter boxes, and barrels set on their sides can also serve as nest sites. Wild Muscovies nest in tree cavities or elevated nest boxes such as those used for Wood ducks; domestic Muscovies will nest just about anywhere, as long as it's somewhat dark and secluded.

## PROTECTING YOUR FLOCK WITH FENCING

Secure fencing is the raiser's first line of defense against a variety of predators. Fencing also keeps your flock from wandering off your property and from invading duck-prohibited zones such as your newly planted vegetable garden. Take a trip to your local feed or building supply store, and you'll encounter a bewildering variety of fencing material: chicken wire, electric wire fencing, woven-wire field fence with graduated openings, chain-link fencing, welded wire of all gauges and heights, nonclimb horse mesh, light electric poultry mesh, and more.

What does a confused duck farmer choose? Wild predators tend to go for prey that's easily obtained, so think in terms of making it as hard as possible to reach your ducks. For starters, surrounding your property with tight woven-wire field fencing, sturdy horse mesh, or chain-link at least five feet in height will help ward off wandering dogs and hunting coyotes, especially when combined with electric hotwire fencing. Dogs and coyotes will gladly crawl or dig under fences, so make sure your fence reaches the ground (you may

*The sturdy boundary fence in the background helps keep this duck flock safe from roaming dogs, coyotes, and other predators. It also ensures that these ducks don't waddle out onto the busy road.*

need to bury the bottom part of it), and regularly check the fence line for holes. An inside buffer fence, if you can manage one, provides additional security. Avoid leaving gaps around or under gates and pen doors where predators or ducks can squeeze through.

Inner fences employed only to contain, separate, or exclude your ducks can be shorter (two feet in height would suffice), unless you keep a breed adept at flying. The heftier duck breeds don't jump as high as chickens do. Electrified plastic poultry mesh works well to confine your ducks during rotational grazing on pasture, when you want to easily move the flock from area to area. If you keep ducks that excel at flying, such as bantam or ornamental breeds, cover their enclo-

*This raccoon may look adorable, but he's also smart, agile, and omnivorous—meaning he won't turn his nose up at eggs, ducklings, or even adult ducks if he can get them easily. Protect your flock with secure housing and pens, especially at night.*

## CLEANING AND MAINTENANCE

Design your flock's house and yard with ease of cleaning in mind. For instance, it should be located conveniently close to a water spigot and the shed where you stash sanitation equipment and litter. If you have to enter to clean it, the house should have enough head room so you won't knock yourself silly on a roof support. Picking up after your messy flock may not rank as one of the most pleasant chores you'll ever do, but it's an important one that will help prevent disease and parasite transmission. It will also keep the country air on your farm smelling fresh. Cleaning methods for duck houses vary depending on how many birds are kept in the house and how big a mess they make.

sures with aviary or game bird netting. Installed over the top of a duck yard, netting has the added benefit of helping prevent losses to aerial predators such as owls and eagles.

When fencing duck yards, beware of chicken wire: it's not very strong and tends to sag, making it a poor choice for predator protection. Combining small-diameter (one-half-inch) chicken wire with a sturdy, larger-gauge welded wire works well for keeping out rats, weasels, and raccoons that will reach inside to snag sleeping fowl. Whatever fencing you choose, make sure the wire gauge of your fence is appropriate for the ducks you keep. Field fence may hold Muscovies, but it won't keep a Call duck from slipping through. Ducklings require special caution—they squirm through amazingly tiny openings and often can't seem to find their way back home.

*Not the greatest job in the world, but someone has to do it. Duck houses and pens require regular cleaning to keep odors and disease at bay.*

# Keeping Your Ducks Safe from Predators

The list of potential predators that may dine on ducks, ducklings, or eggs is depressingly long: fire ants, rats, snakes, snapping turtles, crows, seagulls, hawks, owls, eagles, opossums, raccoons, skunks, weasels, mink, foxes, cats, coyotes, dogs, and more. Declaring all-out war would quickly drain your resources; prevention is your best bet.

- Tuck your birds into a secure house or pen at night, which is when many predators emerge to hunt. Reduce the gauge of your wire, if needed—rats and weasels can squeeze through one-inch chicken wire in a flash.

- Don't leave dog and cat food or uncovered garbage outside, where it attracts raccoons and other varmints. Keep duck feeding areas as clean as possible.
- Keep your property off limits to wandering canines by installing a good boundary fence.
- Conduct frequent security checks of fences and pens to look for signs of digging or holes that would allow a hungry intruder easy access.
- Keep vulnerable ducklings safe in an indoor brooder or completely enclosed pen until they grow large enough that they won't be tempting prey for crows, rats, and cats.

## Daily, Weekly, and Monthly Upkeep

If you have time each day, you can opt for spot cleaning, then follow up with complete removal and replacement of the litter once a week or monthly. Another popular technique used for ducks and other livestock is the deep litter system. It involves regularly stirring up the old bedding and adding a fresh blanket of litter over the top. The shavings, hulls, or straw mingled with duck manure at the bottom begin to compost, generating heat that helps keep the birds warm during winter. Once a year, usually in the summer, the whole works is shoveled out and left in a pile until the composting process is complete. This nitrogen-rich soil amendment can be used as mulch for your garden (see "Making Manure Compost").

## Annual Maintenance

The yearly muck-out is also a good time to give the house a thorough hosing and scrubbing with warm, soapy water to remove dirt and dried manure. Follow this up with a disinfectant or sanitizer used according to directions. Rinse all surfaces well before allowing birds access, allow to dry, and you're ready to start piling on the litter again. It's

## Did You Know?

No fencing is 100 percent predator proof. Wouldn't it be nice, then, if your birds had a burly backup bodyguard protecting them from predators around the clock? Enter the livestock guardian dog. Shepherds have long used guardian canine breeds like the Maremma Sheepdog, Anatolian Shepherd, and Great Pyrenees to safeguard sheep and goats from coyotes, wandering domestic dogs, and other predators. Some duck keepers have also had success employing livestock guardian dogs. Keep in mind, however, that these animals—which are predators themselves—need specialized upbringing and training to be effective.

## Duck Ponds

When most of us think of farm duck ponds, we imagine a pool of sparkling, clean water ringed with cattails and flowers and alive with bright-eyed, quacking ducks.

In the real world, ducks produce copious droppings, flatten vegetation with their big feet, and spend their days dabbling and drilling for yummy worms and other edibles in the dirt, turning it to mud. Set a flock of ducks loose on a little pond that has no inlet, outlet, or pump and filtration system, and you'll have a mucky mess in no time, as mud and droppings accumulate. Build a poorly designed and difficult-to-clean artificial pond, and you'll eventually have the same problem. Your idyllic duck pond will not only become an eyesore and a source of unsavory odors but may also pose a health threat to your feathered friends.

extremely important to clean and disinfect the house when changing over flocks, too.

Duck yards also need cleaning. If you use sand or pea gravel as a substrate, a brisk raking is all it takes to rid the pen of manure and feathers. To conserve sand, you can drill small holes into a big shovel head to make a nifty sifter that captures droppings and debris while letting the sand fall through. Check feeding and watering areas regularly to see if the sand needs changing; moist sand mixed with feed becomes black and foul-smelling, not to mention unsanitary. The pen's substrate should be changed completely as needed—usually once a year.

*The dabbling Mallards on this natural lake couldn't be happier. The lake has an inlet and an outlet, which help maintain decent water quality.*

A natural lake or pond can work well for ducks, provided there's an inlet and an outlet to refresh the water and the water quality is good. Be careful not to overstock; one source lists 100 birds per acre of water as the absolute maximum. If you choose to build a pond, keep in mind that a permit may be required before you can construct one on your property; contact your Natural Resources Conservation Service and local government offices to find out what permits and regulations apply. You'll find them listed in the white pages of your local phone book.

## BUILDING AN ARTIFICIAL POND

You can use concrete to construct a small artificial duck pond, or you can use premolded plastic forms or the tough plastic lining sold especially for ponds.

The pond should be convenient to drain, clean, and refill, and it should have an overflow pipe to prevent flooding. If you run a drainage pipe or hose from the pond into a planted area that needs regular watering, you'll be killing two birds with one stone every time you empty the pond. Make sure the pond has a gradual slope or ramped area where your birds can easily get in and out. Remember that ducks can drown, and ducklings are especially at risk if they're unable to climb out of the water.

Think carefully about the pond's location; you'll want it somewhere within reach of a hose and convenient for duck watching, yet not so close to your house or neighbors' homes that noise and smells are a nuisance. If ponds in your area freeze during

# Making Manure Compost

You can transform the duck manure and yucky litter you clean out of your flock's house and pens into crumbly, nutrient-rich compost to enrich the soil in your garden or apply to pastures. Making compost doesn't have to be complicated or time consuming. The simplest (albeit slowest) method is to pile up the duck doo and litter, along with any other organic matter you want to get rid of, such as vegetable scraps, lawn clippings, and old hay, until it reaches a height of at least three feet. It helps to confine the pile with pallets or a wire cage so it doesn't spread out all over the place. Cover the pile with a tarp so that rain won't wash away the nutrients and bacteria (but make sure the pile stays moist), and then wait. After six months or so, you'll have lovely compost for your garden. For more advanced composting methods, you'll find plenty of information on the Internet or in the gardening section of your local library or bookstore.

# Advice from the Farm

## Housing Your Ducks Properly

The experts share tips on creating top duck environments.

### Summer Freedom, Winter Protection

"I feel that animals are healthier if they can roam relatively freely, eat fresh greens, and catch insects. In summer, my Muscovy ducks run free, using the barn when they want to, but primarily living outside. I recently built a large outdoor pen for peafowl, and in the winter I put the ducks in there. The pen has nylon mesh netting over the top to keep my birds in and birds of prey out. The sides are covered in poultry wire, and there's a three-foot-wide mesh wire on the ground attached to the outside bottom rail in order to keep predators from digging in. The pen contains numerous small shelters for the ducks to get out of the wind."

—Melissa Peteler

### Mess Equals Organic Fertilizer

"I try not to look at the mess [that ducks make] as a negative aspect; instead, I try to manage my duck flock to make it an asset. The ducks are housed in a ten-by-twenty-foot custom duck house all winter in which I use the deep bedding method. I add fresh pine shavings every few days. The old bedding underneath starts to compost, generating its own heat, and by the end of winter it's usually twenty inches deep. During the following summer, I remove the bedding to a compost pile to complete the composting process.

The ducks are in tractors (moveable pens) on a rocky field of dandelions during the summer. The rocky soil keeps them from creating too much mud, and moving them every day also keeps the mess from accumulating. Plus the manure is helping the dandelions be more prolific each year."

—Jenifer Morrissey

### Foiling Bald Eagles

"After losing a number of ducks to bald eagles, I made a large fenced pen and strung Salmon high-test fishing line across it, running the lines about eight feet apart. Then I attached ten-inch-long tinsel tape streamers along each line. The eagles and hawks were actually screaming at me—they wouldn't come down. Last year, all the babies hatched out and nobody was eaten."

— Howard Carroll

### Kiddie Pools for Ducks

"Living in Kansas, it's a fact of life that there are few natural bodies of water, so my birds all have to be provided with a pool of some sort. What I've found works extremely well, and what is used by many breeders throughout the United States, are plastic kiddie pools. They can be found all spring and summer at any number of retail stores and are relatively inexpensive. The depth works very well for ducks; the size is suitable for one bird up to ten to fifteen birds. They're easy to maneuver and can be moved around a lot to prevent mud holes. The pool's

height provides easy access for most adult ducks, while a brick on the outside and one on the inside is all that's needed for smaller ducks or ducklings. These pools can be modified to add drains and hoses so that the water can be directed toward plants, trees, and bushes. I use a circular saw to drill one-inch holes in mine and use a stock tank plug so that when I want to empty them, I simply remove the plug and let the water flow out."

—Cat Dreiling

### Dandy Duck Pens

"Allow more square footage in houses and yard space than you think you'll need. Sand makes an excellent drainage medium in pens: it keeps the birds cleaner and prevents some disease problems. Pen security is vital—heartbreak comes to those keepers who underestimate the local predators."

—Lou Horton

### Ducks and Chickens Together

"Except when they're all outside in the summer, I don't keep the chickens together with the ducks because the ducks muddy the water and mess up everything so the chickens get wet and muddy feet and have no clean water to drink."

— Kate Morreale

### Herding to Safety

"Ducks are wonderful because they're creatures of habit, and they have a very strong flocking instinct. They're much easier to herd than chickens, which tend to scatter. [To keep them safe from predators], we train our ducks to go into their house at night. If they haven't gone in on their own when it's time, we just clap our hands and herd them in. The lead duck runs in and the rest make a desperate dash to follow. They're a little like lemmings."

—Angie Pilch

winter, keep in mind that domestic ducks—particularly Muscovies—are prone to frostbite on their feet. An aerator that keeps part of the pond ice free can help prevent this. If you keep Muscovies, your best bet is to take away their swimming privileges during freezing weather.

To reduce mud around the pond's edges, try spreading gravel or sand and planting sturdy vegetation such as irises and cattails. Again, keeping duck numbers down and rotating access to the pond helps reduce mud formation and gives waterside plants a chance to grow.

## DUCK POOLS

Contrary to what many people believe, domestic ducks can get along fine without a pond, natural or artificial. What they do need at the very least, however, is ample drinking water in a container deep enough for them to dip their heads in to clean their eyes and nostrils. Shallow, three-gallon hard plastic containers do just fine; two per flock of four

*The rocky bank of this idyllic farm pond will help prevent mud formation and erosion as the ducks trek in and out.*

*A sturdy, shallow, three-gallon plastic water container makes a nice—albeit petite—drinking or bathing pool for this Muscovy female. It's simple to clean and easy to move around.*

to six birds is usually sufficient. The containers are available at feed stores and are easy to scrub clean and move when the area around them gets too muddy or soiled with droppings. They're also large enough that most ducks can stand in them and take a partial bath.

Your birds will be happier and their plumage will stay cleaner, however, if you can provide them with more spacious bathing arrangements. Plastic kiddie pools make great duck ponds (see "Advice from the Farm"). They come in several sizes and are fairly easy to move and clean (you'll need to change the water frequently). To give your ducks a way to get in and out of the water, you can either install a ramp or place two concrete blocks up against the side of the pool, one block on the inside and the other on the outside, to act as steps.

If you live where winters turn frigid, the following items can save you time and energy spent hauling water from the house to your flock: a frostless water hydrant with short length of hose that you can easily drain; a stock tank de-icer to place in your birds' water source; and a bubbler to keep a portion of the duck pond ice free. All of these items can be purchased at your local feed store. Hardware stores and pond supply stores might also carry them.

Now that you know what your flock requires for an outside refuge, let's take a look in the next chapter at what your ducks need to keep them healthy and happy on the inside.

# CHAPTER FOUR

# The Duck Diet

While dining on a slime-coated slug or fat grub may sound nauseating to you, to a duck, those foods rank as *haute cuisine*. Like their wild relatives, domestic ducks are omnivorous and love foraging for a wide variety of creepy-crawly fare such as slugs, worms, mosquito larvae, beetle grubs, and snails. Ducks relish both aquatic vegetation, such as duckweed, and terrestrial vegetation, such as grass, and crave many of the same crops we do: corn, tomatoes, blueberries, lettuce, grains, and more. Ducks eat fish and frogs and will even snatch a mouse or bird on occasion. It's precisely this ability to scavenge for their own chow and efficiently convert a variety of feedstuffs to meat and eggs that makes these fowl so valuable to farmers around the world.

A small duck flock allowed to roam where there is abundant natural forage costs much less to feed than does a confined flock that needs purchased, concentrated rations. The drawback is that a flock subsisting solely on forage will probably not grow as fast or produce as many eggs as one raised on a nutritionally complete commercial diet. In reality, most keepers of small flocks, unless they raise their birds in complete confinement, take the middle road when it comes to feeding. Many encourage their ducks to hunt for their own vittles part of the day or year while also providing the birds with supplemental feed to meet nutritional requirements and to keep the flock productive.

There's no one right way to feed ducks that fits all flocks and all situations. In addition to checking out the excellent resources at the end of this book, ask other experienced duck raisers about what they feed their fowl—particularly

*Omnivorous ducks love foraging for a wide variety of food items, including aquatic bugs and plants, grains, berries, snails, and slugs. This little duck flock is grazing on tender pasture grass and no doubt looking for creepy-crawlies.*

those whose birds look healthy and fine feathered, breed well, and live long, productive lives. If you can, consult a veterinarian or extension expert in your area who is familiar with waterfowl. In the meantime, here are some basics about duck nutrition and diets to get you started.

## DUCK NUTRITIONAL REQUIREMENTS

The feed you toss to your ducks must provide them with good nutrition so they will have the energy they need for such essential activities as feeding, digestion, breathing, walking, reproduction, and body temperature maintenance. The diet must supply nutrients such as protein that allow the birds to develop healthy feathers, muscle, bones, and eggs. Given an inadequate diet, your ducks' health, growth, and productivity will suffer. To reach their potential, ducks need to obtain the following nutrients and supplements from their diets in balanced amounts.

## PROTEIN

When a duck ingests protein—from some nice plump beetle larvae, for instance—its digestive system breaks this nutrient down into amino acids. Amino acids are critical building blocks in the synthesis of proteins. The duck can use them to make up the proteins it needs for the formation of muscle and nerve fibers, feathers and skin, and eggs. But not all amino acids are alike. Essential amino acids can be obtained by the duck only through its diet, whereas nonessential amino acids can be produced by the animal itself. Protein quality varies from source to source, and one diet source alone won't supply all the amino acids a duck

*The feed you offer your flock must provide them with the balanced nutrition they need to grow, produce eggs and meat, breed, and live healthy and happy lives. A good feed will provide the proper amounts of protein, fat, carbohydrates, vitamins, and minerals.*

# General Duck Feeding Tips

- **Buy fresh, quality feed, and avoid storing it too long**. Poultry feed is perishable; its nutrients deteriorate, and it can spoil if stored too long. Check the expiration date, and try to finish the bag within three weeks of that date (or even sooner during hot weather, which can hasten spoilage). If you have only a few ducks, buy smaller amounts of chow more often rather than stocking up on large quantities. Use all feed before adding a new bag; if leftovers seem moldy or musty smelling, toss them out and clean the container before adding new feed.

- **Store rations properly in a cool, dark, dry place**. Put feed in a clean container with a tight lid that will keep out disease-carrying rodents and mold-promoting moisture. Metal trash cans work well for thwarting mice and rats but may cause moisture to condense inside. Plastic cans are easy to clean but can be breached by determined gnawing. Use whichever type fits your storage situation best.

- **Clean feeders, waterers, and feeding areas regularly**. Keep dining areas clean to discourage rodents and reduce mold formation. Regular washing of feeders and waterers will help keep your flock healthy. Make sure containers are unbroken and are leak free.

- **Provide feeder space for all your birds**. Whether you use chicken feeders or thrift-store bowls and pans, make sure there's space enough at the feeders to allow all your ducks to eat without being picked on by dominant birds.

- **Use treats to train and tame your ducks**. Offered in small amounts, a favorite food such as whole wheat bread or scratch works wonders to facilitate and maintain your friendship with your flock. The tamer your birds are, the easier it will be to capture and handle them. You can also use treats to lure the ducks into their safe house each night.

- **Make drinking water available at all times**. Ducks offered feed but no water can actually choke. Waterfowl go through more water than chickens do: they not only drink more, they also splash around in it and dip their food- and dirt-caked bills in it. Your ducks aren't trying to annoy you; this behavior helps them clear their air and nasal passages. Check water containers morning and evening to see if they need to be cleaned and refilled.

needs. Consequently, you'll see a number of protein sources, such as fish, bone, meat, and soybean meals, in formulated poultry feeds. Grains such as wheat and milo also provide protein.

## CARBOHYDRATES

Ducks use carbohydrates, found in sugars and starches, as fuel to give them energy for flying, foraging, breeding, egg production, and bodily maintenance.

*This cracked corn is packed with carbohydrates that provide fuel for activities such as flying and breeding. Keep in mind, however, that overloading your ducks with corn can make them fat.*

Unlike the chambered stomachs of ruminants such as the goat, a duck's simple stomach is incapable of digesting large amounts of fibrous material. That's why waterfowl feeds are based primarily on carbohydrate-rich grains such as corn, oats, wheat, and milo—not fiber-packed hay.

## FATS

Dietary fat provides a concentrated source of energy and serves as an energy reserve. It contains fatty acids important for vitamin and calcium absorption, nerve impulse transmission, and tissue structure. Corn oil, soybean oil, and other fats contained in formulated feeds also help eliminate dust and improve taste.

## VITAMINS

Although needed only in small amounts, vitamins are critical to healthy growth, nervous system function, metabolism, and reproduction. A deficiency of these organic compounds can cause a wide range of health problems, from poor blood clotting and nervous disorders to death. Vitamin overdoses are also bad news. Important vitamins are C, A, and D and the family of B vitamins. Commercial feeds usually contain supplemental vitamins not present in the constituent grains and meals themselves.

## MINERALS

Inorganic dietary nutrients needed by ducks include calcium, phosphorous, iron, magnesium, zinc, iodine, and salt. Calcium and phosphorous are macrominerals, meaning that they're required in larger quantities than are trace minerals such as copper and iron. Like vitamins, minerals must be balanced to maintain good health. For example, calcium and phosphorous in the appropriate ratio contribute to strong bones and egg shells. An excess of calcium, however, can lead to kidney problems (see "Grit and Oyster Shell" for the correct percentages of calcium for laying and nonlaying ducks). Calcium carbonate, iodized salt, copper sulfate, and other compounds supplement the mineral-poor grains in commercial diets.

## WATER

Too often taken for granted, water ranks as the most essential nutrient of all.

Water performs a number of life-giving bodily chores: it ferries feed through the digestive tract, eliminates waste products, regulates body temperature, and makes up 90 percent of blood volume. Offer your flock an ample supply of clean drinking water each day.

## GRIT AND OYSTER SHELL

As mentioned in chapter 1, ducks possess a gizzard that does the work of teeth, grinding consumed feed into an easy-to-digest form with the assistance of tiny pebbles and coarse sand called grit. Free-roaming ducks will ingest most of the natural grit they need while foraging and dabbling, but you'll definitely need to offer confined birds insoluble granite grit, which you can purchase from the feed store.

Feed stores also sell crushed oyster shell for laying fowl, to provide the extra calcium they need to produce eggs with strong shells. If you feed a commercial diet, check the breakdown of nutrients on the bag's label: the feed may already contain enough calcium for your laying birds (they need approximately 2.8 percent calcium).

Keep in mind that an excess of calcium can be detrimental to a duck's health, so don't offer oyster shell to

*One of my Muscovies takes a long drink of clean, fresh water— probably one of the most important nutrients she'll consume today. I empty and refill my flock's drinking water tubs morning and evening.*

*As of this writing, if you want to bring up your ducks on commercial organic fare, you'll need to procure an organic chicken feed or a general poultry feed such as this.*

need to thrive, let's look at the four main feed options available.

## COMMERCIAL DUCK DIETS

Chicken folks have it easy: step into any feed store around the country, and you'll find balanced commercial feeds made for chicks, laying hens, and meat birds. Some stores even carry organic chicken feed. For duck raisers, it's a different story. In many areas, finding a nutritionally complete feed prepared especially for ducks can pose a challenge.

Still, it's worth doing some detective work to find a quality commercial waterfowl diet, especially if you're a neophyte duck owner. Complete diets take the guesswork out of feeding, plus they're

nonlaying birds unless their feed is deficient in this mineral (check the feed label; these ducks require only about 0.8 percent calcium).

## OTHER SUPPLEMENTS

When used according to directions, a powdered vitamin and electrolyte supplement made for poultry can benefit both new ducklings and ducks that are ill, geriatric, or stressed. Probiotics, the good bacteria that make yogurt such a healthy food, may also help your birds ward off disease. Look for both products at feed stores and poultry supply companies.

## FEED OPTIONS

Now that you have an idea about which nutrients and supplements your ducks

## Did You Know?

While experts warn that adding other foods to a complete ration can cause an unhealthy imbalance of nutrients, in practice, many raisers do treat their ducks to garden and kitchen goodies, from bread heels to berries. Avoid offering your ducks spoiled, sugary, fatty, or—if you keep layers—strongly flavored foods such as onions and garlic that may impart their flavor to eggs. Similarly, a fish-heavy diet can affect the taste of duck meat. Chopped dark leafy greens and hard-boiled eggs make healthy additions to any duck's diet. Offer extras—particularly bread and other starchy foods— in limited amounts: too much of these items will ruin your ducks' appetite for their more nutritious fare.

## Daily Feeding Routine

The daily feeding and watering of a small flock of ducks is the essence of simplicity. Each morning, I release my little flock of Muscovies and chickens from their enclosed pen and, as I toss out a bit of bread and scratch, take a good gander at them, searching for any signs of sickness or injury. Meanwhile, the ducks perform their morning ritual, greeting one another with hisses, soft squeals, and tail wags. My two favorite girls waddle over so I can spoil them a bit, hand feeding and stroking them. After that, it doesn't take me long to dump some feed in their dishes, rinse and refill their water pans, and—during summer—flush and top off their kiddie pool (during winter, freezing weather means hauling water out, which adds a few more minutes).

At dusk, I check that all fowl have gone into the pen (sometimes my female Muscovies prefer to perch high up in the fir next door) and close them in, safe and secure for the night. A quick water and food check, and I'm done with ducks for the day.

scientifically formulated to provide ducks with the proper ratios of all the essential nutrients they need to stay healthy and produce well.

If local feed stores don't carry duck feed, ask if they can order some. If you're willing to pay a bit more, you can also order waterfowl rations online through a feed supplier such as Mazuri and through some hatchery or poultry supply companies. Follow the suppliers' instructions on how much feed to offer your flock. See the Resources section at the back of this book for more feed suppliers.

## DO-IT-YOURSELF DIETS

If you keep a lot of ducks or can't locate commercial waterfowl feed, concocting your own duck ration out of ingredients gleaned from the feed store may save you some money. Wheat, whole oats, cracked corn, meat and bone meal, iodized salt, oyster shell, commercially prepared vitamin premixes, and other components can be combined to form a healthy feed for your flock. Some raisers even have their duck rations custom mixed, ground, and formed into pellets at a feed mill. Converting the mix to pellets prevents picky ducks from choosing their favorite grains and wasting the rest.

Creating a custom duck diet isn't easy. You can't just throw ingredients together any which way or pick a couple of your flock's favorite food items (such as corn) and leave it at that. Be aware, also, that some feedstuff used for other

*Before you create a custom duck feed for your flock, do your research: it's essential that your birds receive a balanced diet. Having your custom feed extruded in pelleted form, as shown, usually results in less waste.*

animals, such as rapeseed meal and peanut meal, can even be toxic for ducks under certain circumstances. Your birds need the appropriate nutrients in the right balance; no one food item will provide all their nutritional requirements. Keep in mind, too, that their dietary needs change as they grow. The following sections give nutritional requirements by age and stage. For instance, a laying duck must consume plenty of calcium to produce all those eggs, but an excess of calcium in a growing duckling's diet can harm its skeleton. While you don't have to be a poultry nutritionist to make feed for your ducks, it's critical to have some knowledge about duck nutrition or to at least know where to go to get the accurate information you need.

For starters, you'll want to pick up a copy of Dave Holderread's book *Storey's Guide to Raising Ducks,* which gives detailed formulations for making home-made duck feed. This helpful book is listed, along with several other excellent resources, in the Recommended Reading list in the Resources section.

## GRASS-BASED DIETS

Animals reared in pasture-based systems can indulge in natural behaviors such as basking in the sunshine, breathing fresh air, and foraging for grass and other goodies, such as weeds and bugs. And here's a major plus: the animals generally have more room to move about and exercise. This is a far cry from the restrictive lives led by factory-farm livestock. Proponents of grass-based livestock farming contend that the meat and eggs from their fowl are tastier and healthier than are those of factory-farm fowl.

*Pasture-reared ducks like this Muscovy female can forage for much of their own food. Proponents say birds raised in grass-based systems produce tastier, healthier eggs and meat.*

# Pellets, Crumbles, or Mash?

Commercial poultry feeds come in three forms: extruded pellets of various sizes; crumbles, which look like tiny rock chips; and fine mashes. In general, ducks waste less pellet feed than they do crumble or mash. Mash in particular can adhere to wet bills and end up wasted in the water container as the duck dabbles and rinses. Ducks tend to eat more and grow faster when offered a pellet diet (most pellet fare is too big for new ducklings, but you can moisten it with water first). If mash is all that's available, try mixing it with water to make it mushy but not too sloppy before serving it to your flock.

Pasture-raised poultry are usually kept in one of two ways: in portable tractors— small, enclosed pens with open bottoms that the farmer moves once or twice daily to fresh pasture—or in free-range situations, in which they roam a fenced pasture by day and stay in a house at night. By using electric poultry mesh or other temporary fencing, the raiser can rotate the birds through smaller pasture sections, allowing grazed areas to recover.

If you provide the right rotations (moving the flock before they mow the grass below three inches or so) and proper pasture management (mowing, liming, and reseeding as needed), your ducks can glean much of their diet from pasture as they dine on tender grasses, dandelion leaves, chickweed, and insect treats. You'll probably still need to supplement this fresh forage with commercial or homemade feed, particularly as plants go dormant in late fall and winter.

Make sure that your ducks' feeding grounds are free of toxic pesticides, fertilizers, and herbicides. The ducks, for their part, will enrich the soil by depositing their nitrogen-rich droppings as an ecofriendly fertilizer.

## OTHER POULTRY FEEDS

If you lack pasture, can't find a commercial duck diet, or feel uncomfortable mixing duck rations from scratch, don't panic. Poultry feeds formulated for chickens, turkeys, or game birds can also work for duck flocks, although some dietary modifications and additions may be necessary because these birds have slightly different nutrient requirements (see the Recommended Reading list in the Resources section for some excellent sources of nutritional information). For example, ducklings need more niacin than chicks do, or they can suffer from leg problems. If possible, avoid feeding your flock broiler starter

# Advice from the Farm

## Duck Diet Tips

Our experts discuss what they feed their ducks.

### Pleasing the Picky Eaters

"Our ducks are picky. They turn their beaks up at regular farm grain mixes. They'll eat all-purpose poultry pellets, and these have a sufficiently high level of protein for them. We mix it with some cracked corn—that's their candy. They like green leafy stuff; we feed them leftover lettuce from the garden and cut grass clippings. They won't eat spinach at all. They love frogs and slugs!"

—*Angie Pilch*

### Recipe for Good Health

"I feed my Muscovies a commercial duck and goose feed and also give them cooked table scraps, including meat, as they're not vegetarians. In the summer, I come upon grasshoppers while working outside, and I'll give them to my ducks. My ducks seem to be pretty healthy, and I think the most important thing is good, clean food and water. They mess up their water, but I change it twice a day. They can get along without bathing water, but they must have clean drinking water!"

— *Melissa Peteler*

### Custom Feed and Winter Water

"I feed my adult ducks custom rations based on the ones in Dave Holderread's first duck book (*Raising the Home Duck Flock, 1978*). Over the course of the year, the ration changes from holding

to breeding to laying. I chose to go the custom route because I prefer that my ducks have whole grains and fish meal to more closely simulate their natural (and naturally omnivorous) diet. There also seems to be less waste with a whole grain mix. I feed mash to my ducklings. It's a nonmedicated chick starter from the same mill that mixes my feed, with five to seven pounds of brewer's yeast added per 100 pounds of feed so the ducklings get the niacin they need.

Providing water is interesting, especially in this climate, where it rarely gets above freezing in winter. During the winter, I use plastic jugs with openings cut in them. I can beat the ice out of them if I need to, and if they spring a leak, they're easily and cheaply replaced. This winter, I set a bucket in the deep bedding of the duck house, with a second bucket nested inside it. Because the bedding stays warm, I can lift the inner bucket out

each day and empty, clean, and refill it. During the day, the ducks have access to black rubber tubs of water. The black rubber and regular dabbling helps keep the water from freezing solid. I empty the tubs each night. The ducks love their morning swim, even when temperatures are subzero."

— *Jenifer Morrissey*

*Fresh, Quality Feed Is Essential*

"Only a fool invests good money in breeding stock and then 'cheaps out' in feeding them. If at all possible, get feed especially made for waterfowl. The brand of feed is less important than the quality of the ingredients and freshness. Vitamin packages in feeds lose their potency within a matter of a few months or so."

— *Lou Horton*

or other feeds not formulated for waterfowl that contain antibiotics and other added medications; some of these can harm ducks.

## NUTRITIONAL REQUIREMENTS BY AGE

To ensure that any type of ration—commercial duck, homemade, or other poultry feed—is appropriate for your birds, you should understand what your ducks require in the way of nutrition at various ages.

## NEW AND GROWING DUCKLINGS

Newly hatched ducklings need plenty of calories, more protein than mature ducks need (about 18 to 20 percent total), sufficient niacin, and a calcium to phosphorous ratio of 1:1. Their feed must be in a form that tiny beaks can handle, such as crumbles, mash, soaked pellets, or dry pellets no longer than one-eighth of an inch. It's recommended that ducklings receive this starter diet for the first two to three weeks (we'll talk more about feeding ducklings in the next chapter).

Fast-growing ducklings from about three to eight weeks of age will experience a slower growth rate if switched to a 15 to 16 percent protein diet during this time. This lower protein grower diet can help reduce the incidence of wing problems such as angel wing

*These Muscovy ducklings are foraging for vegetation, insects, and slugs. However, they also require a concentrated feed with sufficient niacin and adequate protein.*

(read more about this in chapter 6) and leg problems associated with speedy growth, such as lameness. Producers who want fast-growing meat birds often stick with the higher protein fare until the birds are ready for slaughter at around eight to twelve weeks of age.

## MATURE DUCKS

Somewhere around the nine-week mark, a duck's dietary needs change again. From this point on, except during breeding or laying, feed them a maintenance diet that contains about 14 percent protein. Don't give them feed meant for layers—it has more protein and calcium than they need. Ducks that you keep as pets, rather than as layers or breeders, can stay on this 14-percent-protein diet to maintain a healthy weight.

## NUTRITIONAL REQUIREMENTS BY BREEDING STAGE

A duck's nutritional requirements also change during its breeding stages—the times during which the bird mates, lays eggs (if it's a female, of course), and undergoes its postnuptial molt.

## BREEDING BIRDS

About two to four weeks before breeding season starts, begin feeding breeding ducks a breeder ration with about 17 percent protein. Commercial waterfowl breeder diets such as Mazuri are formulated to provide balanced nutrients that promote breeding performance, hatching egg numbers, and the development of healthy ducklings without making

ducks fat. Keep feeding this ration until egg laying has stopped.

## LAYING BIRDS

Laying ducks whose purpose is to produce eggs for eating also need plenty of protein and calcium while pumping out all those lovely eggs. Commercial layer diets contain approximately 16 to 17 percent protein and 2.5 to 3 percent calcium (the nutrient levels are slightly different from those in a breeder diet). Offer these birds some oyster shell if their diet provides insufficient calcium. As with breeder diets, start your flock on this ration two to four weeks before laying season commences, and keep feeding it until all laying halts.

## MOLTING BIRDS

When feathers start flying far and wide during molting periods, many raisers

*To sustain production of all those beautiful eggs, these laying ducks require more protein and calcium in their diet than do nonlaying adult birds. Look for a commercial diet with 16 to 17 percent protein and 2.5 to 3 percent calcium.*

offer their birds a small amount of cat kibble for added protein (the amino acids help build feathers). Adding oats can also supply extra protein.

## NUTRITIONAL REQUIREMENTS DURING COLD AND HOT WEATHER

Because ducks don't hibernate, they need plenty of carbohydrates from their feed to help them stay warm and active on frigid winter days. If you live in a cold climate, you'll probably notice that your flock consumes more chow during winter. Many farmers offer their flocks a limited amount of energy-rich cracked corn or scratch grain mix, both available at feed stores, to help them weather the cold (be careful—too much corn can make ducks fat).

During hot weather in summer, laying ducks often require increased protein in their diet to keep up production,

as they tend to eat less. Remember to check their water sources regularly, as their water consumption may also go up on sweltering days.

---

### Toxic Mold

Mold produces toxins that can harm a duck's internal organs, muscles, and respiratory system. To keep your flock safe, follow these dos and don'ts:

- Don't feed moldy bread, produce, leftovers, or grain.
- Do store your flock's feed in a container where it will stay clean, dry, and preferably cool.
- Don't give your birds more high-moisture foods (that is, wet mash or table scraps) than they can consume in a day. Remove any leftovers.
- Do check that feed grains have been properly dried before storing them.

## FREE CHOICE OR SET AMOUNT?

Ducklings and growing ducks should be fed on a free-choice basis—that is, allowed to dine on their rations throughout the day and eat all they want. Whether you offer your mature ducks their rations as free choice or as a set amount of feed at scheduled feeding times (usually twice a day) will depend on how you manage your flock (free range or in confinement) and whether freeloaders such as pigeons and crows pose a problem.

How much your ducks will eat—or need to eat—depends on many factors, including their size and age, the season, and how active they are. If you use a commercial diet, check the label for suggested feed amounts, and keep in mind that ducks consume more than chickens do. While it isn't necessary to weigh your ducks, pay attention to your flock's general condition and food consumption. Are your ducks so fat they can barely waddle? Do you notice prominent keels or poor plumage, indications that your birds may not be getting enough food? Is your flock leaving loads of grain at the end of the day for the rats and raccoons to gorge on? If so, consider reevaluating how much chow to dish out.

# CHAPTER FIVE

# Breeding Basics and Duckling Care

Ducklings are one of the biggest perks of raising ducks. They're soft, fuzzy, and too cute to believe—and it should be easy for your duck flock to produce some, right? Just toss some ducks of the opposite sex together, wait for eggs to start appearing and ducks to start sitting, and a mess of ducklings should be the end result—eventually.

Not so fast. First of all, getting eggs is one thing (like chickens, female ducks will lay eggs whether a male is present or not); getting *fertile* eggs and successfully hatching them out is another thing entirely. The strategy described above may work with some broody breeds such as the Muscovy and the Mallard, but with other breeds, it won't. The Indian Runner, for instance, may lay loads of eggs for you to eat, but ask it to sit on those eggs for a whole twenty-eight days? Forget it!

Second, even easy-to-breed ducks shouldn't be allowed to reproduce out of control, with no thought on your part as to what you'll do with all those adorable babies—which, by the way, grow up fast! Will you raise the ducklings for meat or sell them to others to eat? Will you market them as slug-killing pets or as breeding or show stock? Supply ducklings to feed stores? Please don't assume you'll just give the ducklings away to friends and neighbors who want them on a whim (often pressured into the decision by their kids). And whatever you do, *don't* plan to release your surplus stock at a park pond or lake thinking they'll take care of themselves (they won't—see the box "Who Let the Ducks Out?").

It makes good sense, before embarking on a breeding program with any form of livestock, to decide on your objectives and what traits are important to you. Do you want to breed lovely exhibition birds of a certain color, produce more *duck à l'orange* for the table, replace your older layers, or preserve a threatened breed? Knowing your goals ahead of time is critical to your success as a breeder.

## BREEDING FLOCK BASICS

Whatever your breeding objectives, try to start out with breeder ducks that show good vigor and—if they're purebreds—appropriate breed conformation. Obtain specifics on conformation and breed standards by checking out the APA's Standard of Perfection and the breeder association Web sites listed in the Resources section.

The birds should be healthy and neither too fat nor too thin. Avoid breeding any ducks with genetic flaws, and make sure your birds are fully grown before using them as breeders; an immature duck's first eggs are small and less likely to be fertile. In general, light- and middleweight ducks reach sexual maturity at about seven months of age, while heavier ducks can take up to a year. Ducks are at their breeding peak from one to three years of age,

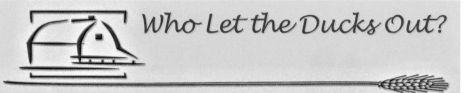

Visit any public park pond or lake, and you're bound to encounter domestic ducks scrambling for bread with the wild Mallards and Canada geese. They're probably not farm escapees— most domesticated ducks, even those that fly, tend to stay close to home when offered plenty of food and protection from predators. More likely, some no doubt well-meaning people had more ducks than they knew what to do with or decided they didn't want ducks anymore and released them, feeling confident the birds would revert to an independent wild state or survive off treats tossed by visitors.

Sadly, the free life isn't always a bed of roses for feral ducks (that is, domestic ducks that have reverted to a wild state). They face dangers seldom encountered on the farm, such as winter starvation; abusive humans; and numerous predators, from domestic dogs to eagles. Worse still is the impact feral ducks have on other ducks and the environment. Breeding out of control, they foul water bodies and urban lawns with their abundant droppings. They hybridize with wild ducks and transmit diseases such as duck plague and fowl cholera. Florida, which has a problem with feral domestic Muscovies, prohibits the release of domestic birds.

If you have too many ducks, don't just let them out; take time to deal with your problem responsibly by controlling overbreeding with diligent egg removal and by finding appropriate homes for your unwanted birds.

*Dandy Duck, my Muscovy drake, displays the vigorous good health you want to see in a breeding bird. He has fathered a slew of ducklings on my farm over the past five years or so.*

although they can successfully breed for longer.

Domestic ducks readily interbreed, so if you keep more than one breed and want to avoid producing hybrids, separate them at least three weeks before the onset of the mating season. Mating will typically start in the early spring, although the timing may vary with climate and latitude. A breeding pair will continue to mate even while the female lays her eggs, so you should prevent the breeding groups from mixing until the ducks complete their clutches and begin to incubate.

## MALE TO FEMALE RATIO

The ratio of drakes to ducks in a breeding flock is an important consideration. Breeders of ornamental "wild" ducks, such as Mandarins, Wood ducks, and Mallards, generally keep these birds in pairs within separate enclosures. Usually monogamous in the wild, these ducks tend to be territorial. With domestic ducks, it's a different situation. Raisers of domestic ducks often keep one drake for each two to six females. Not only are more males unnecessary, but too many can lead to stressful and possibly life-threatening "raping" of the females and fighting among competitive males. Muscovy drakes are especially prone to getting into vicious brawls over their girls. When setting up breeder pens, avoid crowding your birds to keep competition for mates and nest sites to a minimum.

*Drakes, like these two brawling Call ducks, may fight over females during the breeding season. That's why duck raisers often keep a breeding group ratio of one drake to two to six females.*

## ENCOURAGING BREEDING

To maintain your breeders in good condition and increase their reproductive success, offer your mating ducks a breeder feed ration about one month before egg production starts up (see chapter 4).

Dirty eggs make for poor hatching success, so keep pens as clean as possible, and make sure your ducks have their choice of secluded, protected nest boxes littered with straw, wood shavings, or other soft materials (see chapter 3). Fresh litter, changed as needed, will help keep the eggs clean and also insulate them from the cold ground on chilly days. Sometimes you can persuade the females to lay their eggs in the nest boxes you provide by placing a dummy egg in each nest. Try any of the following: golf balls, marked hard-boiled eggs (changed regu-

larly, so they don't rot), sand-filled plastic Easter eggs, or artificial chicken eggs (available from feed stores). But don't be surprised or offended if your ducks drop their eggs just about anywhere; many domestic duck breeds and individual ducks have had the instinct to nest and brood bred right out of them.

If you allow your ducks to roam free part-time, be aware that they may nest almost anywhere on your property that offers a sheltered, secluded site. Muscovy females, hole-nesters in the wild, excel at hiding their nests in hard-to-find spots, such as underneath an outbuilding, behind a stack of hay bales, or in the dim corner of a barn. If you suspect a duck has a hidden nest and would like to find it, try playing detective: watch for when she takes a break from egg laying or incubation to

*Muscovy females such as this pretty girl can be especially sneaky about hiding their nests. Hole nesters in the wild, they may seek out hidden spots in barns, under decks, or in dense vegetation.*

feed or bathe, and nonchalantly follow her back to her nest.

Finally, provide your breeding ducks with plenty of fresh drinking water and, if possible, a bathing pool deep enough for them to float in. While some domestic duck breeds can mate on the ground without a problem, heavyweight ducks in particular often need the buoyancy provided by water to facilitate mating. Water also allows the ducks to cleanse away the sticky, bacteria-rich saliva left on their heads during mating.

## HATCHING OPTIONS

Once your ducks start laying eggs, you have two hatching options available: natural incubation by the mother duck or another broody bird, and artificial incubation in an incubator machine. Each method has its pros and cons.

The simplest way to hatch out ducklings—and the method that yields the highest egg hatchability if you have a good broody bird—is to let a female duck do the incubating of her own eggs for you (if she's willing, that is). After breeding commences and a broody female duck finds the ideal nesting spot, she scrapes and hollows out a simple depression in the litter with her beak, body, and feet. Every day or so, usually during the night or early morning hours, she'll lay one smooth-shelled egg. For the duration of the laying period, which will depend on the duck's breed and the size of her clutch, the female will still step out and about quite a bit, engaging in all her usual activities.

Each egg, if it's fertile, will contain a cluster of embryonic cells existing in a state of suspended development. Development will continue once the process of incubation is set into motion by the mother duck, a substitute broody bird, or an artificial incubator.

How many eggs can you expect? The final clutch size varies among duck species and domestic breeds: a Mallard will lay a clutch of about seven to eleven eggs, while a domestic Muscovy may lay as many as fifteen or twenty eggs. You'll know your duck has nearly finished laying her clutch when she lines the nest with soft down from her breast. If she has produced more eggs than she can completely cover (prolific Muscovies are notorious for this), you'll need to remove some to either discard or incubate elsewhere. The eggs will have a better hatch rate if they go through incubation in a single layer. According to veteran raiser Dave Holderread, good broody hens will frequently hatch out every fertile duck egg they incubate; by comparison, with artificial incubation, the average hatch rate is 75 to 95 percent of the fertile eggs set.

*It looks to me as if this Muscovy female has lined her nest with feathers and down, meaning she's ready to sit for the long haul. Her eggs will take about thirty-five days to hatch—talk about patience!*

## SETTING DUCKS

Once the duck begins sitting tight, making only occasional, brief forays for food and water, incubation has begun. If conditions are right, she will naturally provide the proper humidity, air flow, and temperature for her egg-encased embryos to develop normally. She instinctively knows when to stand up and allow them to cool off on a hot day and when to hunker down, keeping them toasty warm during a chilly night. Throughout the day, she'll regularly turn the eggs and push them about the nest so they receive an even amount of heat from her body. When she leaves the nest to feed, drink, or bathe, she'll tuck a blanket of down and bedding over her clutch to keep the eggs insulated and hidden.

Breeds that make good setters or brooders include Muscovies and bantam ducks, such as the East Indies and the Mallard. Next best would probably be the Appleyard and middleweights like the Cayuga and the Orpington. Pekins, Runners, and Aylesbury ducks are generally poor setters, but don't rule them out completely—some individuals can surprise you. For Mallard-derivative breeds, the incubation period generally lasts for twenty-four to twenty-nine days. Muscovy ducks sit longer—about thirty-five days or so.

Don't forget about your patient duck during the incubation period; she still needs care and attention. Make sure she has food and water close by so she won't be forced to leave her eggs unattended for too long. Don't place it too close, however; you don't want the food and water to soil the nest and eggs or attract rodents to the site. Nesting ducks normally take occasional breaks. If yours obsessively sticks to her nest, you might need to carefully remove her once a day so she has a chance to feed and drink. Be alert, too, for the bird that seems committed to setting an infertile clutch. You'll need to remove the eggs; if you don't, the duck may sit well past the eggs' expected hatch date, starving herself in the process. Aside from this, try to avoid disturbing her. Consider separating her from the rest of the flock so they won't bother her either.

Keep in mind that a setting duck and her treasure trove of eggs are an enticement to many predators, so it's crucial to ensure that your brooding bird has protection. If she chose to nest

*Notice how protectively this mother Muscovy hovers over her newly hatched brood. Muscovies make wonderful setters and mothers, for their own eggs and young as well as for those of other ducks.*

somewhere other than in a secure house or pen, try placing a covered portable pen, electrified poultry mesh, or a large cage around her, nest and all. Attempts to move a duck and her nest, unless she's nested in an easily transported box with a solid bottom, are usually unsuccessful.

## ARTIFICIAL INCUBATION

It isn't always feasible for mother duck to incubate her own eggs. As I've mentioned, some duck breeds are known for laying plenty of eggs but being poor setters (individual ducks vary, too). Others tend to flunk out in the mothering department. Where nest-raiding predators pose a problem, even good brooders may have difficulty bringing their eggs to the point of hatching. In such cases, you may need to use artificial means to incubate the eggs.

Here's another scenario to consider: A setting duck can cover only so many eggs, but you may want to hatch out

## Helpful Broodies

Muscovy females make marvelous setters and protective mothers, and their large size means they can cover up to fifteen duck eggs. If you have a chicken that goes broody whenever eggs accumulate (Silkies and Orpingtons often make good broodies), she may also be a good candidate for brooding duck eggs. Once she's sitting steadily, simply substitute the eggs you want hatched for the ones she's setting. You may need to mist the eggs with a little warm water occasionally, because a chicken won't supply as much moisture to the eggs as a fresh-from-the-bath duck will. Although some chickens will raise adoptive ducklings after they hatch, many won't, so plan to move the babies to a brooder. And don't forget to thank your broody bird.

more eggs than that from a particular duck—a rare breed, perhaps, or an exceptional exhibition bird. You'll obtain a greater number of fertile eggs if you collect the eggs daily from the laying duck's nest. (The reason is simple: she'll keep on laying, thinking her clutch is not yet full.) Rather than leave the nest empty, you can set one or two dummy eggs in it; otherwise, the duck might think her clutch has been raided, and that could cause her to abandon the site for a new one. The eggs you gather will need incubating, and this is where an incubator can prove its worth.

A third instance in which artificial incubation comes in handy is if you want ducklings without having to breed ducks. In this case, you can order fertilized hatching eggs through the mail and hatch them in an incubator. Hatching eggs can be purchased from some hatcheries and breeders for less than the cost of a live duckling. While most hatching egg sources can't guarantee that the eggs they send you will definitely hatch, they take special care in producing, choosing, handling, and storing the eggs they sell to maximize egg fertility and hatchability.

## Egg Candling

You can verify that the eggs are fertile and check for dead embryos by candling the eggs at about seven days. Most breeders do this; some repeat the procedure once a week until hatching. Candling involves holding and gently rotating the egg against a candling machine or a flashlight in a dark room or closet; this will illuminate the inside of the egg. Your hands should be clean and dry when you touch the eggs, so you avoid clogging up the pores through which gas exchange occurs. Do not dawdle while candling—you don't want the eggs to cool off too much—but don't rush either. Handle the eggs with care, and avoid jarring or shaking them.

During candling, an infertile egg will look pretty clear; you'll see the air space at the large end and a shadowy yolk, but nothing else. An egg with a dead embryo shows a dark line or circle of blood. Take a sniff. Dud eggs give off a foul odor as time goes by, and they can eventually turn into stink bombs, exploding their putrid contents onto the good eggs. Remove the bad eggs and discard them, but handle them gently so they don't burst. A fertile egg will have a dark spot in the center with a web of blood vessels radiating out from it. At about two weeks, the egg beneath the growing air space will look very dark, but you may be able to make out the tiny heart beating and see the embryo moving. Congratulations! If all goes well, you'll have a baby duck.

## Incubators

Incubators commonly used by small flock raisers come in a number of sizes and styles with varying price tags. They range from $20 plastic-domed miniature incubators, the kind often used in schools to hatch out a few eggs, to large, standing cabinet models that accommodate several hundred eggs and cost $700 or more.

Basically, incubators can be divided into two types: still-air and forced-air types. Still-air machines heat the eggs by convection; they lack fans to move the air inside the unit. They're often less expensive and simpler to operate than forced-air units, but it can be much more difficult to

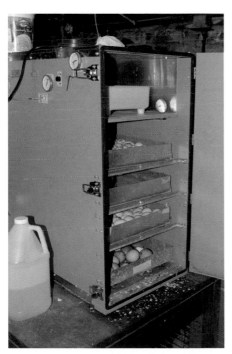

*Incubators come in a number of sizes and styles with widely varying price tags. Here's a nice cabinet model that has four shelves to hold plenty of duck eggs.*

adjust heat and humidity levels, especially for novices. Forced-air incubators come with fans that circulate heated air evenly throughout the interior, helping keep the unit at a constant temperature and humidity level that promotes successful hatching. Many have automatic egg turners and multiple tiered shelves to hold the eggs—thousands of eggs, in the case of the large incubators used on commercial poultry farms.

Follow the manufacturer's instructions for setting up the incubator, and be sure to get it running several days before adding the eggs to ensure that it works properly and to establish the correct settings. The settings may need to be altered slightly depending on your climate, elevation, and other factors; egg incubation isn't an exact science, and it takes practice and experience to be successful at it. Even then, don't expect a 100 percent hatch rate with an artificial incubator.

Set up the incubator in a room where the temperature stays relatively constant. Avoid cold or drafty areas or spots where the temperature and humidity fluctuate, such as near a heater, a sunny window, or an air conditioner.

About six hours before setting the eggs, transfer them from their cool storage spot to a place where they will gradually reach a room temperature of about 70 degrees Fahrenheit. This will keep them from experiencing temperature shock when placed within the heated incubator. Set the eggs on the incubator racks (if provided), with the

*When handling or turning duck eggs, as shown here, make sure to wash and dry your hands to avoid contaminating the shell with dirt and bacteria. Avoid jarring the eggs as well.*

the eggs will also keep the embryos from being damaged or killed by extreme cooling. Make sure your hands are clean and dry when you collect the eggs, and handle them with care. Eggs that have thin or cracked shells or that look abnormally small or large are best discarded.

Despite your efforts, some eggs may still be soiled with dirt or droppings. They'll require gentle cleansing to wash away egg-damaging bacteria before you store or incubate them. If they're only slightly dirty, brush the soiled spots lightly with a clean, rough, dry cloth or a steel wool scrubbing pad. Don't do this too vigorously: it's important to avoid rubbing away the waxy cuticle, or bloom, that covers duck eggs and protects them from bacteria. Although it's possible to wash really grubby eggs with a sanitizing solution, some sources advise against washing the eggs because it can reduce

large end elevated and the small end down. As with natural incubation, you should candle the eggs at seven days to identify infertile eggs or dead embryos and discard them so they don't contaminate the good eggs.

## Preparing Eggs for Incubation

How you collect, handle, and store the eggs before setting them in an incubator has a big impact on their hatchability. The laying bird's environment and nest should be kept as clean as possible to prevent fecal contamination of the eggshells. Checking for eggs twice a day contributes to egg cleanliness and will help you beat predators to the punch. When the weather is colder, bringing in

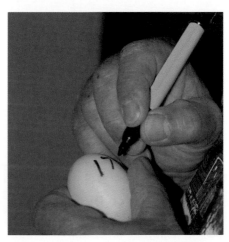

*When gathering eggs for incubation, you should carefully mark them, as shown here, with the lay date, breed of duck, and any other important identifying information.*

hatchability. Before storing hatching eggs, mark the shells with the date on which they were laid, along with breed and individual identification if needed, using a dull pencil or wax crayon.

While you wait to accumulate enough eggs to set under a broody or in the incubator, store the eggs in a cool place such as a basement, cellar, garage, or pantry where the temperature stays a constant 50 to 60 degrees Fahrenheit (refrigerators are too cold). Moisture loss can negatively impact hatchability; the humidity during storage should ideally be 75 percent. You can store the eggs rounded side up and small side down in egg cartons with their lids cut off. If possible, store the eggs no longer than a week before setting them; the hatch rate declines the longer the eggs sit in storage. Propping up one end of the carton a few inches with a block of wood or brick and switching the block from one end to the other each day will help keep the embryos from adhering to the sides of the eggs, especially if you have to store the eggs for a period of more than a week.

## HATCHING TIME

If you're incubating eggs from a domestic dabbling duck, expect the eggs to begin hatching at about twenty-eight days, give or take a day or two. Muscovy eggs will be ready to hatch at about thirty-five days. Warmer than normal temperatures in the incubator can shorten incubation time, and cooler than normal temperatures can lengthen it.

## Clean It Up

It is vitally important to clean your incubator between hatching sessions to prevent the spread of disease. If you're using a new incubator, clean it before its initial use to remove any dust or chemicals. If it's a used incubator, you will need to clean and sanitize it before you use it for the first time. Follow the cleaning instructions that come with the incubator, or you can use the cleaning procedure offered by the Mississippi State University Extension Service, which is this: First, remove all organic matter (eggshells, feather dust, down, and so on) from the incubator with a vacuum or broom. Then wash it out well with warm water and detergent. In the case of a particularly dirty incubator, you may also want to rinse it with a disinfectant solution such as quaternary ammonia.

About three days before the eggs hatch, you may hear the wonderful sound of the babies softly chirping inside. Double-check that the eggs are in proper position for hatching, with the blunt end tilted up—this is where the duckling will peck into the air space and take its first breaths. You can stop turning the eggs now, or switch off the automatic turner. Watch the temperature carefully, as the ducklings will generate their own heat while they struggle to emerge; you may need to reduce the temperature to keep it at the correct setting.

During hatching, waterfowl eggs require more ventilation than during incubation as well as a slightly higher

For duck embryos to successfully develop in an incubator, the machine (or the duck raiser) has to regulate the following:

*Temperature.* Proper temperature is critical: too much heat, and the embryo will cook to death; too little, and development slows and stops. Most incubators come with a thermometer for monitoring the interior temperature of the incubator, and many have thermostats to set the temperature. In a still-air machine, position the thermometer so it will show you the temperature at mid-egg level because temperature will vary at different heights (it will probably be warmer at the top). A forced-air machine doesn't have this temperature variance. Experts generally recommend that the temperature for incubating waterfowl eggs in a forced-air incubator be 99.5 degrees Fahrenheit. For still-air incubators, some raisers advise a higher temperature of 102 degrees Fahrenheit. It's wise to monitor the temperature several times a day and keep a record to refer back to at the end of the hatch.

*Ventilation.* Developing duckling embryos, while they may not have operative lungs yet, still need oxygen, and they get this through thousands of tiny pores in the eggs' shells. All incubators come equipped with vents that allow fresh air to enter; the vents can also be used to regulate humidity. Forced-air units have fans that increase air flow, dispersing oxygen, heat, and moisture throughout the incubator.

*Humidity.* It's normal for an egg to lose water as the duckling develops and the air cell expands. An incubator must provide enough moisture from water evaporation to prevent the egg from drying out but at the same time allow a certain amount of moisture loss so that the duckling can successfully hatch. Different incubators come equipped with various types of water reservoirs that can be used to supply moisture and regulate humidity. Some also come with a hygrometer, or wet-bulb thermometer, to measure humidity levels inside the incubator (you can purchase one from a poultry supply company if yours doesn't have one). The hygrometer should read between 84 and 86 degrees Fahrenheit, although the correct humidity level varies depending on climate.

*Egg Turning.* Nesting ducks turn their eggs frequently during the course of the day, an action that prevents the embryo from sticking to the side of the egg and increases hatching success. If your incubator has an automatic turner, you've got it made: the incubator will do the mother duck's work for you. If not, you'll need to gently turn the eggs yourself at least three or four times a day. Marking an X on one side of each egg and an O on the other (with a blunt pencil or wax crayon) can help you keep track of which eggs have already been turned.

level of humidity (88 degrees Fahrenheit on your hygrometer, or wet-bulb thermometer, which measures humidity levels within the incubator). If your incubator unit contains a hatching tray, this is the time to carefully transfer the eggs onto it. Try to avoid opening the unit again until hatching is completed because opening causes temperature dips and moisture loss. Many breeders use a separate hatching incubator set specifically for the temperature and humidity required by the emerging ducklings. Hatching is a messy process, and separating out the hatching eggs from the incubating eggs helps keep the latter clean.

Soon the duckling will use the hard egg tooth on its bill to push and peck a hole into the eggshell. Look for this telltale sign of imminent hatching, called pipping, on the rounded end of the egg.

Over the next day or so, the duckling continues to work its way out of the shell, finally emerging wet, bedraggled, and exhausted. Don't worry—after resting and drying off within the incubator for a few more hours, your precocious duckling will be all fluffed out and ready to head to its new home in the brooder with its fuzzy friends. We'll talk about brooders for baby ducks in a minute.

If the duckling has managed to peck a hole in the egg but can't seem to make any more progress over the next hours, you can help it by very carefully peeling bits of eggshell away. If you see blood on the shell membrane, stop and wait a few more hours, then try again. Unfortunately, ducklings lacking enough vigor to complete the hatching process on their own often don't do as well as their stronger brothers and sisters.

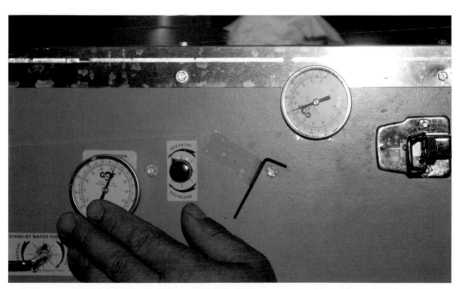

*To help ensure a good hatch, careful monitoring of temperature and humidity within the incubator is essential during the incubation and hatching process.*

## CARING FOR MOTHER-REARED DUCKLINGS

Ducklings left in the care of an attentive mother duck or substitute maternal duck won't require a lot of specialized care from you (although, as in setting prowess, duck breeds and individuals vary as to mothering ability). Of course, the new ducklings need protection from a host of predators, so it's important to house the duck and her young in a maternity pen of some sort that's secure enough to keep large and small varmints out. The pen must also be duckling proof; adventurous ducklings can squeeze through surprisingly tiny gaps and mesh openings. For the first week or so, the mother duck will hover over her babies with wings slightly spread, keeping them warm and sheltered beneath her. Still, it's important that the maternity pen provide the family with shelter from heavy rains, wind, and sun.

Offer the ducklings a waterfowl starter diet that meets their nutritional needs, if possible (see chapter 4). Baby ducks with their tiny beaks need mash, crumbles, or moistened pellets to eat. Place their food in a shallow dish they can easily access, and provide plenty of it, because their mother will help herself to some. Provide mother duck with her own food in a steep-sided dish to keep the little ones out. Ducklings also relish and thrive on tender grass cut into tiny pieces (no long strands) or finely chopped dark leafy greens. Some rotten fruit hung in a mesh bag out of reach of the ducks will lure fruit flies for the hungry ducklings to snack on. Of course, the mother duck benefits from these menu items, too.

*An attentive mother duck such as this Muscovy female will keep her ducklings warm and teach them where to eat and drink. You will, however, have to provide the family with protection from duck-hungry predators. A maternity pen of some sort is a must.*

The ducklings and their mother will also require an ample supply of water to drink, but use caution here. Ducklings can drown in large water containers if they have no easy way to climb or jump out. What's more, the mother duck herself can accidentally drown or crush the ducklings if she climbs into a large pan with them to bathe. Until the ducklings are large and nimble enough to jump out of a water pan, use large, narrow-troughed chicken waterers, and avoid giving the ducklings a container to bathe in. If you can supervise them, however, older babies enjoy going for a swim in a kiddie pool or on a pond where there's ample room and where they can easily exit the pool. Ducklings can quickly become chilled, so schedule swim times for fair weather.

*A mother Muscovy teaches her duckling how to forage for small slugs, tender grass, worms, and other natural delicacies. Make sure your duck family is safe from dogs, cats, and other predators when you let them out to roam.*

Allowing the family out into a safe, grassy area early on will give the mother duck a chance to show her ducklings how to forage. Watch out for farm dogs, cats, or other livestock that might harm the babies. A warning: some Muscovy drakes will kill ducklings, so use caution when these big guys are around.

## CARING FOR BROODER-REARED DUCKLINGS

Ducklings purchased by mail, bought from a feed store, or hatched out in an incubator will need a substitute for their absent mother. A brooder unit provides a warm, nurturing environment for the ducklings to live in until they feather out sufficiently to keep themselves warm. It also gives them a safe haven until they grow big enough to hold their own against other ducks and not be picked off by crows, cats, and rats.

You can purchase a brooder built especially for chicks or ducklings or easily fashion one from a metal stock tank, a

*My Muscovy ducklings pictured here love to make a splash in the kiddie pool with Mom. I'm always careful to supervise their swim parties until they get bigger.*

# Handling Ducklings

With their soft, fuzzy down and high-pitched peeps, ducklings just beg to be held and cuddled. As irresistible as they are, however, remember that ducklings are fragile babies and shouldn't be overhandled. Young children who might not know their own strength should not handle ducklings. If in doubt, hold the baby duck and let the child gently stroke it. Always supervise kid-duckling interactions to prevent tragic accidents.

Direct contact with poultry and their droppings can spread the bacterium salmonella, a common cause of foodborne disease that produces diarrhea, fever, cramps, and sometimes more severe illness. To prevent spreading this bacterium, make sure that all who handle a duck or duckling wash their hands well afterward in warm, soapy water for at least twenty seconds. Tell kids that you're sorry, but no kissing of ducklings is allowed.

sturdy cardboard box, wood box, plastic storage box, or hard-plastic kiddie pool. Setting up and outfitting the brooder before your ducklings arrive or hatch will forestall any frenzied last-minute trips to the feed store. For starters, place the brooder in a convenient, dry, draft-free spot where predators or pets won't

Two of my Muscovy ducklings soak up the warmth of a light bulb in their simple cardboard brooder box.

be able to reach the new babies. Depending on the container's height, you may need to cover it with a mesh top if your ducklings excel at jumping and climbing. If your brooder is fairly small or you have a lot of ducklings, you may have to move your brood into larger accommodations somewhere down the road to avoid unhealthily crowded and dirty conditions.

Outfit the brooder with a thermometer so you can monitor the temperature down where the babies hang out; 90 degrees Fahrenheit is the usual recommendation for the first week, and then you can reduce the temperature by five degrees per week until it reaches 70 degrees Fahrenheit. To supply the proper temperature, the brooder will require a heat source, such as a hanging metal reflector and lightbulb or other

This brooder lamp will stand in for the mother duck, keeping the new ducklings from becoming chilled

type of brooder lamp. A large brooder may need two heat sources. Simply raise the heat source to reduce the temperature. Remember: any heat source can pose a fire hazard if it comes in contact with something flammable, so use caution and common sense.

Allow enough space in your ducklings' abode for them to escape the direct heat of the lamps if needed; however, don't let any ducklings get chilled in the cooler outskirts of the brooder during those first few weeks. You can discourage them from wandering too far from their heat source by using a draft guard or shield, available from feed stores and poultry supply companies. A draft guard is a roll of cardboard 12 to 18 inches high that opens out into a circle and lines the inside of the brooder. It eliminates the corners ducklings tend to

crowd into and cuts down on drafts. The ducklings' behavior will tell you even better than a thermometer would whether the brooder is too warm or too cold. If the babies noisily cram together beneath the light, they're probably too cold. If they constantly stay at the outer reaches of the brooder or, even worse, you see them panting, it's too hot for their comfort.

Some raisers recommend initially lining the brooder not with shavings but with an absorbent layer of paper towels, cloth towels, or sheets. Newly hatched ducklings may ingest shavings along with their food as they learn to dine on their crumbles or soaked pellets. Never keep ducklings on a slippery surface, such as newspaper, because the constant slipping and sliding can give ducklings a condition known as spraddled leg. Within a few days, however, you

If you observe them closely, brooder ducklings such as these will "tell" you if they're too cold or too hot by the way they position themselves relative to the lamp.

# Advice from the Farm

### Breeding Ducks Successfully
Our experts offer tips on growing your flock.

*Breeding Time*

"To help determine how early in the year to separate the (mixed) flocks and start collecting eggs, I learned this tip from another breeder. When the hens first start laying eggs (mine start around February 1), separate the flock into purebred groups. After the requisite three weeks it takes for purebred eggs to be laid, most of the hens will be laying well, and I start collecting eggs then. I install my heated pond—a water trough—about a week before the three weeks are up. My experience has been that the larger breeds really need a pond of some sort for breeding."

—*Jenifer Morrissey*

*Multiple Hatchings*

"I have a two-stage duckling transfer from incubator to brooder because my eggs never hatch all at once. I have a one-square-foot cardboard box with a burlap bag on the floor and its own heat lamp, plus a very small waterer and feeder. I transfer the dried duckling from the hatcher to the box, dipping its beak in the water and food. After about a day, I move the duckling to the brooder. This staged approach helps the youngest ducklings get their feet under them before they have to cope with their older flockmates."

—*Jenifer Morrissey*

A NOON DAY SIESTA

### Still-Air Versus Forced-Air

"Still-air incubators are much less user friendly than forced-air incubators, which is why almost all new machines sold are forced air. This is primarily due to humidity control; it takes someone with experience to adjust a still-air incubator to the right humidity. Newbies would be much better off beginning with a forced-air machine to give them more chance of immediate success."

*—Lou Horton*

### Bringing Up Ducklings

"We put the ducklings in a high-sided bin with a terry towel on the bottom, a brooder lamp, organic chick starter, and fresh water. The towel prevents the ducklings from straddling. After two weeks, we allow the ducklings to swim supervised in a kiddie pool for about fifteen minutes. We set up another kiddie pool (without water) in the house with the brooder lamp, canvas on the bottom, food, and water. They stay as our house guests until about eight weeks of age. By that time, they're so messy and get everything so wet from playing in their waterer, we move them out into a stall in the barn. They remain in the stall until they're too big to fit through our fencing."

*—Dawn Turbyfill*

### Fighting Drakes

"I keep only one [Muscovy] male around, as multiple males will fight over one female and will even drown her if they try to breed her in water. One male gets on top of her to breed, then more pile on, and she doesn't stand a chance. I once pulled a dead female out of a stock water tank."

*—Melissa Peteler*

### Easy Ducklings

"Ducklings are very easy to care for. Get them under a light for warmth, with feed, clean water, and litter. It's important that they have a nonmedicated feed. To start with, we give them water in chick waterers. When they get bigger, we give them a big rubber dish with a rock in the middle so they can easily get out."

*—Bryon James*

should lay down a thick layer of litter material, such as shavings, chopped straw, or sawdust. Although ducklings are adorable, they do have wet, smelly droppings, and they seem to relish mixing and spilling their food and water. Translation: be prepared to change their litter often to keep it clean, relatively dry, and free of mold.

Your ducklings will need shallow feeders large enough to allow them all to eat at the same time. Their feed, offered free choice (see chapter 4), should be a proper starter ration that includes sufficient protein and niacin, with grit provided on the side. Warning: ducklings gobble a lot of food—definitely more than chicks do—and grow fast! Like ducklings raised by their mother, your brooder babies will benefit from some finely chopped grass or dark greens in addition to their commercial fare.

A constant, ample supply of water is also essential, but be sure to provide the ducklings with water containers that they can't jump into. Plastic chick waterers with narrow troughs work well. Save swimming for when they're older and can do it outside of the brooder. The warm, moist environment of a waterfowl brooder leads to the rapid growth of mold and the proliferation of bacteria, so again, clean the feeders and waterers frequently.

*Small chick waterers with narrow troughs like this one, which I use for my new Muscovy babies, will help keep small ducklings safe from drowning accidents that may occur in regular water pans.*

*These fast-growing Muscovy ducklings love hunting for slugs and bugs in our backyard; the exercise and natural forage is great for them, and they're great for my garden. I've seen them gobble surprisingly large, slimy slugs with relish. Go, ducks!*

When the sun shines, try to get your sheltered ducklings out into a safe outdoor pen where they can graze on young grass, hunt for bugs and worms, swim under supervision, and maybe even see the big ducks. They'll love the exercise and environmental stimulation, and you'll love watching their antics. By the time they're one month old, the ducklings will have grown in enough feathers to keep them warm outside in all but the most inclement weather. Of course, they'll require shelter and protection from predators, just as adult ducks do. Before you know it, your ducklings will have reached their two-month birthday and will essentially be adult ducks.

# CHAPTER SIX

# Flock Health and Handling

A flock of healthy, happy ducks is a joy to behold: tails a-wagging, they greet the day with enthusiasm—cavorting in their swimming pool; preening their sleek, glossy plumage; searching bright-eyed through the grass for delicious bugs. When your animals are the picture of good health, life on the farm feels right. Even on a cloudy day, it seems as if the sun is beaming down.

For those of us who have become completely enamored with our little flocks, that feeling of well-being changes drastically when a duck falls ill. You notice one morning that Daisy doesn't come speed-waddling over for breakfast with her companions. Instead, she sits in the back of the house looking listless, feathers ruffled. Suddenly it seems as if a black cloud has blocked out the sun. How sick is she? What's wrong with her? Will the rest of the flock catch whatever she has?

Happily, waterfowl tend to be hale and hearty creatures when given proper care. But even the most conscientious management won't guarantee that your birds will never get sick or injured. In this chapter, we'll look at proper ways to handle ducks in sickness and in health. We'll also cover basic information on some of the health problems your flock can experience. For a more in-depth treatment of the subject, read some of the books recommended in our Resources section, or visit the Web sites listed. In addition, see appendix B, "A Glance at Common Duck Diseases," for a handy list of the most common duck afflictions.

## DISEASE PREVENTION BASICS

Let's begin our discussion of flock health with an important question: How do you prevent illness and injury from ruining your ducks' day—and yours—in the first place? Let's look at some savvy strategies for minimizing problems.

## CHOOSE GOOD STOCK

Start with healthy stock from a reputable source. Whether you choose to build your flock with ducklings or with adult ducks, try to obtain your birds from a good source that you know carries healthy stock. If you are picking out the ducks yourself—at a feed store or a farm, for example—choose ducks and ducklings that appear vigorous and active. Avoid those with pasty rears, discharge from the eyes, or leg problems as well as any listless-looking birds that just sit around with their eyes closed all the time.

*This pretty Call duck pair gliding on a pond look bright-eyed and in good feather: they'd be a good bet for starting a healthy flock.*

## Duck Health Statistics

**Average deep body temperature**
107.8°F or 42.1°C

**Mean heart rate**
190 beats per minute

**Average respiration rate**
8–12 breaths per minute

*Source: Avian Physiology by Paul Sturkie, Cornell University*

## MAINTAIN A GOOD DIET

Feeding your birds a healthy, balanced diet with ample fresh water is critical. An inappropriate or unbalanced diet ranks as one of the leading causes of health problems in domestic ducks. Ducks can't thrive on a diet of bread alone—or corn or lettuce or grass—any more than we can. Overdoses, deficiencies, and imbalances of specific nutrients can be bad news for your flocks' health (see chapter 4). Waterfowl also require an abundant supply of clean drinking water to remain healthy. With ducks' dabbling and bathing habits, keeping their water sparkling clear all the time is impossible, but do change it at least once or twice a day, and scrub the containers regularly to keep the water from turning foul and stagnant.

## MAINTAIN PROPER HYGIENE

Avoid crowding your ducks. Ducks are social animals, but they don't enjoy being packed like sardines. Overcrowding causes filthy conditions, promotes the spread of disease, and increases aggression and stress. So ditch the factory-farm mentality, and give your ducks plenty of space to breathe, bathe, eat, preen, interact, and basically behave like ducks.

Keep your flock's housing, pens, and swimming pools or ponds as clean as you can. We've said it once (or twice) and we'll say it again—ducks are messy creatures, especially when confined in small houses and pens rather than being allowed to roam a larger area. Regular cleaning of your flock's abode, dining spot, and enclosures will cut down on parasites, disease-carrying flies and rodents, and harmful molds and bacteria (see chapter 3 for cleaning techniques and litter recommendations). It will also prevent your ducks from experiencing the sheer stress—and thus lowered immunity—that comes from living in a filthy, foul-smelling environment. You should also clean or flush your flock's bathing facilities regularly to decrease health risks associated with stagnant, dirty water.

## PROTECT DUCKS FROM OTHER ANIMALS

Control pest populations and keep your ducks away from wild birds. Rats, mice, crows, and pigeons drawn to a leftover buffet courtesy of your ducks can bring disease and parasites. So can the migratory waterfowl alighting on your pond and the pretty wild birds flitting about feeders. If possible, use fencing or enclosures to bar your ducks from areas frequented by wild waterfowl; these birds pose one of the biggest disease risks to your flock. You should also prevent access to the ground around your bird

*Migratory waterfowl, such as this wild Mallard female and her ducklings, can transmit disease to your flock. If possible, use fencing to bar your ducks from areas used by wild waterfowl.*

feeders where droppings accumulate. Control rodents as much as you can, but with common sense and caution; you don't want your ducks or pets ingesting poison or getting caught in a rat trap (see the box "Advice from the Farm").

## KEEP A CLOSED FLOCK

A closed flock means that no new birds enter until it's time to replace the flock completely. It also means that all the resident birds stay put—no going back and forth to shows or fairs to mingle with other waterfowl and poultry. Closed flocks are standard procedure on large commercial poultry farms, where biosecurity is a big, big deal. Obviously, not every small duck farmer can—or even wants to—keep his or her flock completely closed. Still, think carefully before saying, "Sure, why not?" when your neighbors offer you their last two ducks (hey, what happened to the rest, anyway?) or when you're tempted to take a few free surplus fowl sitting in a cage at your local feed store. Some birds come with stuff you didn't bargain for, such as infectious diseases and parasites.

## QUARANTINE NEW OR SICK BIRDS

If a closed flock isn't an option for you—for example, you regularly purchase or exchange breeding stock or you love to show ducks—then put new or returning ducks through a quarantine period before mingling birds. Even fowl that look completely healthy can harbor disease, and some illnesses have long incubation periods. Keep new birds isolated from the rest of your flock for at least four weeks. Ducks back from the fair or show should stay in quarantine for a minimum of two weeks. Have a separate set of cleaning equipment, feed dishes, and other paraphernalia for each group of birds (or sanitize well before exchanging supplies), and take care of your resident flock *before* tending to the quarantined

## Did You Know?

Although commercial poultry operators routinely utilize vaccines to prevent various contagious diseases, raisers of small duck flocks are much less likely to vaccinate their fowl. Why? Poultry vaccines usually come in vials with enough doses to treat thousands of birds, and they must be used up in a short period of time. In addition, few vaccines are available for ducks. For raisers of small flocks that experience relatively few disease problems, vaccinating may seem to be an unnecessary expense and chore.

Vaccination of small flocks is needed only if you've had disease problems in the past, if outbreaks have occurred in your area, or if you frequently show your ducks or acquire new stock. Before embarking on a do-it-yourself vaccination program, call your state diagnostic lab veterinarian or a local poultry extension specialist to find out what vaccines—if any—are recommended in your area. If you must inoculate your flock, ask your veterinarian or an experienced duck keeper to show you how to administer the vaccinations correctly.

*A duck returns from a show. Birds can pick up diseases at shows. The returning ducks should be placed in a quarantine area away from the rest of your flock for a minimum of two weeks and watched carefully for signs of ill health.*

posing of any dead birds promptly and properly (see the box "Disposing of Deceased Ducks").

## Keep Their Environment Safe

A strand of wire dangling loose off the fence, a sharp nail protruding from the duck house wall, shards of broken glass, a bottle cap, a hole into your ducks' enclosure large enough for a raccoon or mink to squeeze through—all these hazards can spell disaster. When caring for your ducks each day, survey their environment: If their bin of feed smells moldy, chuck it. If a bald eagle is hunting overhead, you may need to revamp your duck yard or management techniques to keep your flock safe. If you spot a clump

birds. Any fowl showing signs of an infectious disease should be promptly removed and isolated from the rest of the birds for observation, diagnosis, and possible treatment.

## Be Biosecure

With highly pathogenic avian influenza a looming threat (see the box "Ten Facts About Avian Influenza" on page 106), biosecurity is definitely for our birds and not just for commercial operations anymore. Biosecurity encompasses measures that keep infectious diseases off your farm, including the strategies outlined above. Other sensible measures include restricting visitor access to the area where you keep your ducks (especially bird-owning folks); using a disinfectant foot bath; changing your clothes and footwear after you've visited another farm, a fair, or an auction; disinfecting poultry cages and equipment that have been to another farm or the fair; and dis-

*Be sure to regularly check pen fencing, as I'm doing here, for holes that might allow a predator to enter or a duckling to escape.*

Sadly, all of us who keep ducks must face the day when we lose a duck to old age, disease, an accident, or a predator. What then?

"Most states have laws about disposing of dead animals, so make sure you obey local laws and ordinances," says Richard Fulton, DVM, PhD, an avian pathologist at Michigan State University. "In most states, burial on personal property is usually an option. Dead animals should be buried at least three feet below the surface, or wild animals will dig them up." For one or two birds, he adds, disposal in the garbage is usually another option. To eliminate flies and odors, double-bag the duck in plastic garbage bags and tie them off before placing them in the garbage container. Larger commercial farms either incinerate dead birds on site or remove them to landfills for burial.

of baling twine in the grass, ready to snag a duck leg, pick it up immediately.

## RECOGNIZING ABNORMAL BEHAVIOR

While duck keepers should know the warning signs of ill health or injury in their birds, learning each duck's normal appearance and behavior is just as important. Ducks may not be as obviously individualistic as dogs or horses, but they often have different personalities, even within the same breed. Some are shy, others outgoing and friendly; one top duck always rushes the food dish first, another bird at the bottom of the pecking order hangs back. You may discover that your birds' behavior changes during the course of the year: a normally active, vocal duck becomes subdued while molting; a friendly quacker turns aggressive when she hatches her brood.

Be a good observer of your ducks when they're healthy, and you'll find it easier to quickly identify any abnormal behav-

*If this Pekin duck didn't come out to eat with the flock, it would set off a warning bell in an experienced duck raiser's head— especially if the bird was looking lethargic, with feathers fluffed.*

iors or signs that indicate ill health or injury. Give each of your birds a bill-to-tail inspection at least once a day, and really focus on its appearance and behavior. In general, a healthy duck has smooth, glossy feathers except during molting periods; bright, discharge-free eyes and nasal openings; a clean vent area; and a good appetite. A vigorous duck will take baths throughout the day and spend time preening, foraging, drinking, and sleeping.

The runny eye and matted feathers on the face of this Pekin duck could indicate an eye infection, respiratory illness, or other disease. A consultation with a veterinarian would be your best course.

## SYMPTOMS AND WARNING SIGNS

Many domestic animals, like their wild kin, instinctively take great pains to hide sickness or injury so they won't be seen as easy prey, and ducks are no exception. Signs of illness in birds may be subtle and difficult to spot, so vigilance is important. The following symptoms should set off warning bells in your head: coughing, sneezing, gasping, nasal or eye discharge, sluggishness, depression, ruffled feathers, watery or bloody diarrhea, poor appetite, an unusual loss of feathers, abnormal drop in egg production or soft-shelled eggs, swelling of head and neck, purple discoloration of exposed skin, tremors, drooping wings, incoordination, twisting of head and neck, and any sudden deaths. Indications of injury are usually more obvious: limping, a drooping or oddly bent wing, a closed eye, the presence of blood.

## WHAT TO DO WHEN A BIRD IS ILL

Death or any of the illness symptoms listed above could indicate infectious disease. Your first step should be to isolate the affected duck from your other birds right away. Place the patient in a warm, dry, well-bedded cage, dog kennel, or other small enclosure with food and a water and electrolyte mix, which you should always have on hand as part of your duck first aid kit (see the box "Duck First Aid Essentials"). Keep noise and stress to a minimum.

Ducks showing signs of sickness should be isolated from the rest of the flock in a dry, well-bedded cage or pen such as this one.

Although it may be tempting to try to diagnose the disease and treat the bird yourself with feed-store medications, your duck will have a better chance of recovery if you seek professional help—consult with your local veterinarian, cooperative extension office, diagnostic lab, or the state veterinarian. In some cases, the survival of your entire flock may depend on it. Duck diseases can either be contagious (infectious) or noncontagious. Noncontagious diseases, such as aspergillosis, will usually affect only a few ducks and won't spread among birds. Contagious diseases, such as avian influenza, can

## Ten Facts About Avian Influenza

1. Many avian influenza (AI) strains occur worldwide in birds; most of these strains cause little or no illness in domestic poultry or humans.
2. Experts divide avian influenza viruses into two types: low pathogenic (LP), which usually causes minor symptoms, and high pathogenic (HP), in which mortality in poultry can approach 100 percent.
3. AI is normally spread by direct contact between birds, from equipment or cages contaminated with droppings, through respiratory secretions, and by migratory waterfowl.
4. Symptoms of HPAI in poultry include sudden death (no clinical signs), a drop in egg production, coughing and sneezing, diarrhea, swelling of the head and combs, lethargy, and purple discoloration of legs, wattles, and combs.
5. Domestic ducks can carry HPAI without showing clinical signs.
6. One strain of highly pathogenic avian influenza, the Asian strain of H5N1, has infected and killed poultry—and more rarely humans—in Asia, Africa, the Middle East, and Europe. Most people who fell ill had direct contact with infected poultry or their secretions and droppings.
7. Like the human flu, avian influenza viruses mutate easily and often. Experts contend that H5N1 could eventually exchange genetic material with a human influenza virus to create a highly transmittable virus capable of causing a flu pandemic.
8. The AI virus is easily killed with regular soap, sunlight, bleach, and proper handling and cooking of poultry meat and eggs.
9. Good sanitation, preventing your flock's contact with wild waterfowl, and other biosecurity measures can help keep your ducks from contracting this disease.
10. If you experience unexplained illness or sudden deaths in your flock, call your local extension service or an avian veterinarian.

sweep rapidly through a flock; for such cases, seeking help in determining the cause is especially critical.

A phone consultation with the vet can help you avoid some costly mistakes. For instance, it may be tempting for you to administer an antibiotic yourself. However, using an antibiotic will not cure a viral disease, may cause resistance in bacteria when used improperly, and could even kill your duck if it's the wrong kind. If only one or two ducks take ill, don't automatically treat the entire flock as a precaution unless your veterinarian instructs you to do so. Treat only the sick birds.

## OTHER HEALTH THREATS

Ducks can also become ill from poisons and parasites. The following sections provide some preventive measures to help keep your flock healthy.

## POISONS

Foraging ducks seem to either instinctively steer clear of poisonous plants or avoid consuming enough of these plants to do them any harm. But when given no other edible options, ducks may eat toxic plants. For a list of such plants in your area, contact your local extension agent or visit http://www.aspca.org/toxic plants.

Ducks can also accidentally ingest some poisons. For example, rodent poisons and insecticides can be highly toxic to ducks; read directions carefully before using these in areas frequented by your flock. Take steps to restrict animal

### Duck First Aid Essentials

When injuries or illness strike, time is usually of the essence. To avoid a frantic trip to the feed store or veterinarian's office, keep the following first aid items on hand so you'll be prepared for emergencies:

- Antibiotic ointment and antiseptic spray
- Gauze, first aid tape, and cotton balls
- Insecticidal poultry dust for mite or lice infestations
- Pet carrier for transport
- Plastic storage or tackle box to store all these items
- Probiotic powder
- Quarantine cage or enclosure
- Scissors
- Styptic powder to stop bleeding
- Veterinarian's phone number
- Vitamin and electrolyte mix for poultry
- Wooden Popsicle sticks or tongue depressors (for splinting)

access to these poisons, or better yet, find safer alternatives.

Botulism, another deadly form of poisoning, occurs when ducks dine on toxins produced by the anaerobic bacterium *Clostridium botulinum*. Stagnant bodies of water or decaying plants and carcasses that provide optimum conditions for this bacterium are usually the culprits. The disease causes paralysis, and infected ducks die within one or two days. Your best bet for prevention: bar

Stagnant water bodies can be a source of botulism, a deadly form of poisoning. If your ducks have access to a pond such as this one, make sure you keep it as clean as possible.

pealing organisms are a fact of life for our birds and for us (parasites make up the majority of species on our planet). Parasites affecting livestock usually fall into two categories: ectoparasites, such as mites and lice, which live on the outside of an animal's body; and endoparasites, or internal parasites, such as roundworms and coccidia, which spend part of their life cycle inside the animal's body.

While many parasites are fairly benign, others can cause health problems in birds, ranging from itching to severe anemia. Creepy-crawly lice plague poultry by biting, sucking blood, or dining on skin scales; they can cause intense itching, weight loss, and poor growth. Tiny relatives of the spider, mites tunnel into the skin to lay eggs or lay them at the base of feathers; they can also cause

your ducks from stagnant water, and keep pools and ponds clean.

Aflatoxin poisoning occurs when ducks eat grains or seeds that have been contaminated by aflatoxins produced by several types of mold, usually the result of wet harvest conditions. Again, never give your flock moldy feed, bread, or bedding. Castor bean poisoning and poisoning by high levels of erucic acid in rapeseed (canola) meal have also been reported in ducks. Ducks that frequent ponds at or near hunt clubs where lead shot is used often suffer from lead poisoning. For cases of suspected poisoning, contact a veterinarian as soon as possible to discuss treatment options.

## PARASITES

Parasites are organisms that live and feed off other organisms, providing no benefit in return—freeloaders, basically. Whether we like it or not, these unap-

Ducks and mold don't mix: never feed your flock moldy grain, bread, or other food items. Toss out wet leftovers, especially on warm days, and clean feed dishes regularly so they don't become a breeding ground for mold and bacteria.

*Excessive biting or scratching can signal a parasite infestation. External parasites such as lice can cause intense itching, weight loss, and poor feathering.*

weight loss and lead to death from anemia. Good hygiene will help control these ectoparasites, as will providing your flock with proper bathing facilities. You may need to use a commercial insecticide formulated for poultry, such as an insecticidal dust, if your birds have a heavy infestation. Always read labels and follow the manufacturer's directions before using these products.

Internal parasites of ducks and other poultry include gapeworm, large roundworm, tapeworm, capillary worm, and coccidia. Mature, healthy animals generally develop a degree of immunity to internal parasites, whereas young and old animals and those under the stress of breeding, poor nutrition, or overcrowding are more likely to suffer ill effects from parasitism.

Signs that internal parasites are running amok include weight loss, poor growth, reduced egg output, coughing, diarrhea, lethargy, weakness, head shaking, pale membranes from anemia, and even death. Deworming agents, or anthelmintics, to combat various parasites can be obtained from your feed store or poultry supply company, but consult a veterinarian before using these products. Some dewormers are effective against only one type of parasite, and few are approved for use in treating waterfowl. Avoid using dewormers as a preventive measure when your birds don't have a problem (to be certain, ask your veterinary office to check a fecal sample). Unfortunately, the indiscriminate use of these agents has already created dewormer-resistant "super" parasites.

A group of protozoan parasites called coccidia can also cause illness or death in waterfowl, particularly in ducklings. Often present in the soil, these organisms kill cells in the duck's digestive system, leading to watery or bloody diarrhea and a depressed attitude, which you can tell by the bird's ruffled feathers and decreased food consumption. Overcrowded conditions and wet, dirty bedding are major contributors to the problem. While coccidiostat medications are commonly employed to prevent and treat coccidia in chickens and turkeys, caution must be used when treating ducks with these medicines. Waterfowl drink and eat more than other poultry do, so overdosing can easily occur. In general, small duck flocks rarely require medicated feeds.

*A pair of dog nail trimmers can be used to trim overlong duck nails, as shown here. Keep some styptic powder on hand in case you accidentally cut the quick.*

## COMMON LEG, FOOT, AND WING PROBLEMS

Duck legs may look sturdy and strong, but these body parts are actually a duck's weak link. While many chicken farmers will nab their birds by the legs, grabbing a duck this way can result in injury (read about the correct way to catch a duck in the box "Handling Ducks"). Ducks can also injure their legs when chased by a predator or a person. Niacin-deficient diets can cause leg problems in ducklings, and rations with excessive calcium can do the same for growing birds.

Bumblefoot, a condition in which the footpads become cracked and infected, usually affects adult ducks kept on hard, dry surfaces, such as concrete and gravel, or on wire. It can also occur when ducks constantly walk and lie on wet, dirty bedding. A reaction between water and the uric acid in droppings creates ammonium hydroxide, a weak, lye-like solution that can produce burning ulcers on the feet. Prevent bumblefoot by layering hard surfaces with cushy dry litter, by allowing birds access to grassy terrain, and by keeping your flock's accommodations as clean and dry as possible.

While we're on the subject of feet, remember to keep an eye on your ducks' toenails, and trim them if they seem overlong or hinder your duck's waddling. Older Muscovy drakes, in particular, with their long, sharp claws and sedentary lifestyles, may need the occasional pedicure with a pair of dog nail trimmers. If the nails are clear, you'll be able to see where the blood vessel ends to avoid cutting the quick, but keep some styptic powder on hand, just in case. Styptic powder works as a clotting agent to rapidly stop bleeding from nail trimming injuries.

Twisted wing, also called angel wing, occurs when the wing's primary feathers grow up and away from the duck's body. It can happen to one or both wings. More a cosmetic flaw than a health problem, the condition can be inherited or caused by a diet too high in protein. If you catch twisted wing early, try correcting it by realigning the wing and feathers into a proper folded position, then taping them into place with masking tape. Be careful that you don't tape too tightly or block the vent opening. Release the wing after about two weeks. With any luck, your duck will still be able to fly, although probably not as well as a bird that has never had this condition.

Some domestic duck breeds (notably Muscovies, Mallards, and other bantams) are talented flyers; you may wish to ground these birds to ensure that they stay on your property or in their pens, especially if you acquire them as adults. Wing clipping is easy to do, and unlike cutting off a wing's pinion, it doesn't permanently disable birds. While an assistant holds the bird and stretches out the wing, use a sharp pair of scissors to cut the eight or nine long primary or flight feathers on one wing at the level of the smaller secondary feathers. Watch that you don't snip thick, blood-engorged pin feathers that grow in to replace old feathers during the molt. If you are unsure about how to clip wings, ask an experienced duck raiser to show you how to do it so you don't injure your

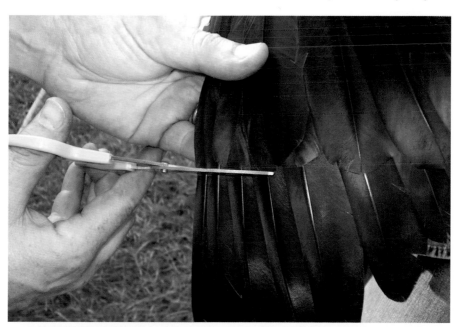

*My husband demonstrates cutting the long outer primaries just ahead of the secondary feathers on one of our Muscovy females.*

# Advice from the Farm

### Flock Health

Our experts share their experiences of managing their ducks' health and safety.

*Tough Duck*

"One day a bald eagle caught one of my Egyptian Runner ducks. It actually had her pinned on the ground, starting to eat her. I scared it away and discovered the duck was alive but had two big holes in her breast; she'd lost a lot of blood. I put Bag Balm in the holes and placed her in a cage in a quiet spot with a heat lamp for a week or two. Amazingly, she recovered!"

—*Howard Carroll*

*Cold Duck*

"Believe it or not, adult ducks can suffer from hypothermia. They become slow and listless and can't walk very well. We always have a large cage, brooder light, food, water, and electrolytes ready, since one has to work quickly to save the duck. I place the hypothermic duck's feet on my hands to gradually start warming the bird—it seems that the feet are their thermostats. I alternate putting my warm

hands under its wings and feet, until the duck starts moving more. I have syringes to gently wash some electrolyte water over the inside of its mouth if the duck shows no interest in drinking right away. They're soon drinking their water shortly after that."

—*Dawn Turbyfill*

You'll need to keep an eye on them until the legs are fully developed at about five months. The only breed we had this experience with was the Aylesbury ducks—it was a lot of work! They're definitely not a breed I'd recommend for the new duck owner."

—*Dawn Turbyfill*

### Duck Wrangling

"When handling ducks, we stop them by the chest or shoulders with both hands, and pick them up supporting their whole body. The chest is nestled in the crook of the left arm, and the body cradled by the hand; the forearm supports the body, almost as if holding a football. This prevents any injuries to the shoulders, wings, or legs."

—*Dawn Turbyfill*

### Safer Rodent Baiting

"Rodent bait stations can be made out of PVC pipe with a T fitting. Insert the pipe into the T, then turn it upside down and put the rodent bait in the stem of the T. Rodents can get to the bait, but your ducks can't. Use chewing baits for rats, and pellet or seed baits for mice."

—*Richard "Mick" Fulton, DVM*

### Niacin Treatment

"Some duck breeds physiologically need more niacin to prevent weak legs. If you don't act quickly, the ducklings will be walking on their knees. Two sources are niacin powder added to the ducklings' water, and brewer's yeast added to their feed. The faster this deficiency is caught and treated, the faster they will recover.

### Good Health in a Nutshell

"Proper care and management will go a long way toward keeping ducks free of disease. Get good stock, don't overcrowd them, provide plenty of fresh water and good quality feed. Overcrowding is the worst enemy of health in waterfowl."

—*Lou Horton*

ducks. Remember to repeat the procedure when new feathers grow in again after the annual molt, or your newly flighted birds may take to the sky.

Many raisers prefer not to clip their birds' wings; they believe that their ducks have a better chance of avoiding predators if they can fly. Once they become accustomed to your farm and know where their food and shelter comes from, most domestic ducks prefer to stick around.

## HANDLING DUCKS

Once in a while, you'll need to catch a duck to treat an injury or health problem, transport it to a show, check its weight, or perform some other task. Untamed ducks can be quite elusive, so make the effort to befriend your birds, bribing them with yummy treats so they'll permit you to approach them closely. Teaching the ducks to enter an enclosed area each day for their meal will make capturing them much easier. It will be less stressful and hazardous for your flock—and you—if you corner them in a small pen rather than embarking on a wild chase around the pasture. A long-handled, medium-size fishing net comes in handy for nabbing shy, fast, or flighted birds in more open areas (such as your neighbor's backyard!). However, extricating ducks from a net is a tricky procedure and almost always messes up their feathers. Whenever possible, it's best to catch them by hand.

First, make sure you dress appropriately for duck catching; wear long sleeves to protect against scratches, and skip your nice clothes because there's a good chance you'll be pooped on. Remember that legs and wings are off-limits for grabbing. Instead, pin the

*Notice that this Muscovy's wings are pinned between my arm and side to forestall flapping. I'm also wearing long sleeves and jeans to prevent scratches from her sharp nails.*

# Transporting Ducks

If you're transporting ducks to a fair, show, or new home, follow these guidelines from the Virginia Cooperative Extension to help your birds reach their destination healthy and alive.

- Transport ducks in escape-proof, well-bedded carriers (tough plastic dog crates or kennels, for example), with openings small enough to prevent the ducks from sticking their heads through.
- Ensure that the carrier has sufficient ventilation and air flow during warm weather, but avoid exposing your birds to drafts on chilly days.
- Don't crowd birds into crates; this can cause overheating and fighting.

- A blanket or towel tossed over the crate helps keep birds calm, but skip this during warmer weather.
- Take along a spray bottle with cool water or some ice packs in case your ducks show signs of overheating. Be sure to offer them water to drink during rest stops.
- Secure the kennels within your vehicle so they won't tip or move during transit.
- Never leave ducks unattended in a parked car or trailer during summer, and don't leave them in a dark-colored crate or unshaded cage out in the sun.
- Avoid subjecting ducks to extreme changes in temperature (from an air-conditioned vehicle to the hot outdoors, for example).

duck's wings against its body with both your hands or—if you can't do this because you have a vigorous flapper or a big duck—catch the bird gently around the neck (don't squeeze, and don't do this with small ducks whose necks are more delicate) to hold it in place until you slip your other hand and arm underneath its body from the front. A captured duck may paddle furiously (Muscovies are especially notorious for leaving vicious scratches), so it's important to get control of the feet with one hand while cradling the bird firmly against your side. If you're dealing with a big duck that might peck at your face, it may be best to carry the bird facing backward.

Here are a few more words of warning: during handling, don't let that duck bill near your face. Ducks are not ferocious animals, but they will peck and bite if provoked, and your shiny eyeball could make a tempting target. After you, your children, or anyone else handles or pets your ducks—even those pristine-appearing downy ducklings—make sure hands get washed well with soap and warm water. Use an alcohol-based cleaner if water isn't available. Even a minor bout of salmonellosis is nobody's idea of a good time.

# CHAPTER SEVEN

# Harvesting the Rewards

B y now, you probably have a pretty good idea of what it takes to provide your ducks with secure housing, a balanced diet, water to drink and bathe in, and proper health care. This last chapter will focus on what ducks give us in return for all the attention we lavish on them and how to make the most of it.

Ducks, as I've already mentioned, are useful and generous creatures. Allowed to roam your property, they help control slugs, snails, mosquitoes, and other pests, providing ecofriendly fertilization services as they go. They trim grass and weeds and control aquatic weeds in waterways. They delight us with their happy-go-lucky attitude and antics and often make wonderful, responsive pets. Who knows? They could even be a boon to our mental health and blood pressure, like those more conventional pets, the dog and the cat.

It's doubtful, however, that humans living 4,000 years ago decided to domesticate ducks primarily because they made cute, friendly companion animals. Rather, they were attracted to these birds for the life-sustaining gifts they offered: eggs and meat.

## DUCK EGGS FOR CONSUMPTION

You won't find duck eggs sitting next to chicken eggs at most grocery stores, and that's a shame. Like chicken eggs, duck eggs are a rich source of protein, choline (an essential nutrient that may help prevent heart disease), and two important nutrients found in the yolk that may guard against vision loss—lutein and zeaxanthin. Eggs contribute to countless dishes and desserts, from quiche to cookies, and they make a terrific convenience food all by themselves. Protected within their shell wrapping, eggs store well under refrigeration for up to two months. They cook up easily and quickly and can be prepared in a number of delicious ways.

Eating eggs in moderation won't clog your arteries with cholesterol, either. According to a press release from Harvard Health Publications, only a small amount of the cholesterol in the food we eat enters our bloodstream. Saturated fats, and those evil trans fats, are the biggest culprits affecting blood cholesterol levels. Dining on one egg a day shouldn't pose a problem for most of us, particularly if we cut back on trans and saturated fats at the same time. If you're still worried, you can always eat the cholesterol-free egg white, or albumen (which consists mainly of the protein albumin and water), and skip the yolk. However, the yolk contains most of the good stuff. You may also find it more difficult to separate yolk from white in a duck egg—they adhere to each other more strongly than do the yolk and white of a chicken egg.

Anyone who keeps laying fowl knows that freshly gathered eggs taste and even look better than store-bought eggs, especially if the birds have been allowed to range and eat a natural, varied diet. The yolks glow a more vivid orange-yellow, the albumin stands up instead of oozing all over the pan, and the eggs scramble to firm perfection. Depending on the bird's diet, fresh duck eggs taste much like fresh chicken eggs; they're perhaps a bit richer and "eggier" tasting. But they do differ in a number of other ways (see the box "Nutritional Comparison of Duck and Chicken Eggs").

*This duck egg is rich in protein and contains important nutrients such as choline and lutein. Duck eggs taste much like chicken eggs but tend to have a firmer texture when scrambled. They also add loft to baked goods.*

## Nutritional Comparison of Duck and Chicken Eggs

|  | Duck Egg (100g) | Chicken Egg (100g) |
|---|---|---|
| Calories | 185 kcals | 147 kcal |
| Protein | 13 g | 12.5 g |
| Fat | 14 g | 10 g |
| Saturated Fat | 3.7 g | 3.1 g |
| Monounsaturated fat | 6.5 g | 3.8 g |

*Source:* USDA National Nutrient Database

For starters, the thick, smooth shell of a duck egg is harder to crack than the shell of a chicken egg; prepare to use more force. Duck eggs also have a yolk that's larger relative to the white and thicker and stickier; this can put some people off. When scrambled or fried, a duck egg has a firmer, chewier texture than a chicken egg does. With the extra protein they contain, duck eggs add fluff and loft to baked goods. Lots of people enjoy eating duck eggs, but if you're considering keeping ducks primarily to provide eggs for your own table, try them first to make sure you like them.

Nutritionally, duck eggs contain slightly more protein, calcium, and B vitamins than chicken eggs do. They also have more fat and cholesterol because of their larger yolks. Interestingly, some people who have allergies to chicken eggs say they can eat duck eggs without a problem (but people can be allergic to duck eggs, too). If you allow your ducks to range, their eggs may be even better for you: some studies have shown a higher level of healthy omega-3 fatty acids in free-range eggs compared with eggs from confined poultry.

## GETTING GOOD EGGS

As you know by now, laying ability varies by duck breed. Prolific layers include the Magpie, Ancona, Harlequin, Runner, and the queen of them all, the Khaki Campbell, which can pop out more than 300 eggs a year. Once you've settled on a laying breed, getting plenty of good eating eggs comes down to following a few simple guidelines, including offering the proper diet (see chapter 4), providing good nest sites (see chapter 5), and confining your flock until nine o'clock in the morning. Ducks normally finish egg laying sometime during the night or early morning. If you coop your free-roaming

*These duck eggs, courtesy of the ducks at Heirloom Heritage Farms in Spanaway, Washington, will keep in the refrigerator for up to two months. But they'll taste better eaten fresh!*

ducks until nine o'clock or later, you won't have to embark on an extensive and sometimes fruitless egg hunt every day. It will also keep egg-loving varmints from devouring the eggs before you find them. Gather eggs promptly in the morning so they don't have a chance to get dirty, and keep the duck house and nests clean with regular litter additions and changes.

## CLEANING AND STORING EGGS MEANT FOR EATING

As noted earlier, eggs have a protective coating called bloom that keeps bacteria from entering the porous shell. Scrubbing and washing removes this coating, increasing the risk of contamination and spoilage. Still, ducks are not the neatest creatures, and dirty eggs happen

even with preventive measures. Badly soiled eggs are best discarded, but you can clean a slightly soiled egg by gently brushing it with a dry cloth or steel wool. If needed, you can wash a dirty egg with warm water and a sanitizer made for that purpose, but store the egg separately and use it sooner than the others, as washed eggs won't keep as long.

Cool eggs as soon as possible. Store fresh eggs pointed side down in breathable cardboard egg containers in the refrigerator. They keep up to two months but will taste much better if used sooner.

## DUCKS FOR MEAT

It's not only ducks' eggs that have been underutilized here in the United States, it's the meat as well. Chicken and turkey products dominate the poultry meat scene, while duck meat, unfairly stereotyped as laden with fat and calories, is generally shunned by much of our diet-obsessed populace.

But humans, including the ancient Chinese and the Romans, have enjoyed duck meat for thousands of years. To this day, domestic duck remains popular in the cuisines of many countries, from Vietnam to France, and for good reason. Ducks multiply quickly, and they're highly efficient at converting forage into meat. Duck meat is packed with high-quality protein as well as significant amounts of certain B vitamins and important minerals such as iron, zinc, selenium, phosphorus, and copper. Although considered a white meat along with other poultry, duck breast meat looks darker in color than does chicken or turkey breast. This coloration is the result of the increased presence of red blood cells carrying oxygen to fuel the duck's flight muscles (chickens and turkeys stand and run more than they fly).

As far as duck fat goes, most of it resides in and under the skin, so if you remove the skin, you'll have a portion even leaner than chicken (see the box "Duck and Chicken Meat Comparison"). A duck of any breed that's allowed to forage and exercise will produce leaner meat than will your typical confinement-raised Pekin duckling. Muscovies and their hybrids are also known for their lean meat. If you've ever sampled expertly prepared duck in a Chinese, Thai, or French restaurant, you'll know that duck is fabulously flavorful, rich, and tender.

## BENEFITS OF HOME-RAISED MEAT

Raising your own ducks for the table has some distinct advantages. You'll know exactly how the birds were raised, knowledge you won't have about poultry

## Duck Egg Trivia

- Got your hard-boiled eggs and raw eggs mixed up? No problem—just give the eggs a spin on a hard surface. Hard-boiled eggs spin perfectly; uncooked eggs wobble.

- If you want to determine whether an egg is fresh, place it in a bowl of water; a fresh egg will sink. As an egg ages, the air space grows, so an older egg floats.

- Duck egg whites have poor whipping qualities compared with chicken eggs. A teaspoon of lemon juice added for each egg white should help.

- 1,000-Year-Old Eggs or Ming Dynasty Eggs, an Asian delicacy, are actually only 50 to 100 days old. A coating of lime, ashes, and salt, plus a 100-day burial, gives the eggs a petrified look.

- *Balut,* another delicacy savored in Asia and said to be quite nutritious, is a cooked fertilized duck egg containing an embryo that is seventeen to twenty-one days old.

purchased from a store—what they ate; where they lived their short lives; and how they were treated, slaughtered, and processed. You can choose what diet to feed your meat flock—organic or conventional—and whether to let them graze in grassy pastures or search for slugs around your garden. You can give them ponds or pools to bathe in and clean, uncrowded houses to sleep securely in at night. You can ensure that their final hour comes with a minimum of stress and pain. In short, you have the opportunity to dine on fresh, farm-raised meat from happy ducks that lived normal duck lives—a definite plus if you (like me) feel guilty if, by purchasing your meat, you encourage the sad existence of factory-farm poultry. What's more, this concern about how the animals we eat lived and died is shared by an increasing number of consumers, particularly in urban areas—something to think about if you plan to market your ducks for meat.

If you intend to slaughter the ducks yourself and have never done so before, ask an expert to come to your farm and

*Young Muscovies search for pesty treats in an organic garden. One of the benefits of raising your own meat ducks is that you know exactly how they were raised.*

## Nutritional Comparison of Duck and Chicken Meat

| Roasted Duck Leg with Skin (100 g) | | Roasted Chicken Leg with Skin (100 g) | |
|---|---|---|---|
| Calories | 217 kcals | Calories | 232 kcals |
| Protein | 27 g | Protein | 26 g |
| Fat | 11 g | Fat | 13 g |
| Saturated fat | 3.0 g | Saturated fat | 3.7 g |
| Cholesterol | 114 mg | Cholesterol | 92 mg |
| Iron | 2.1 mg | Iron | 1.3 mg |

| Broiled Pekin Duckling Breast (Skinless) | | Roasted Broiler Chicken Breast (Skinless) | |
|---|---|---|---|
| Calories | 140 kcals | Calories | 165 kcals |
| Protein | 28 g | Protein | 31 g |
| Fat | 2.5 g | Fat | 3.6 g |
| Saturated fat | 0.6 g | Saturated fat | 1.0 grams |
| Cholesterol | 143 mg | Cholesterol | 85 mg |
| Iron | 4.5 mg | Iron | 1.4 mg |

*Source:* USDA National Nutrient Database

show you how to do this necessary but unpleasant chore in the most humane way possible. Of course, not all of us duck raisers can stomach the thought of butchering our feathered friends ourselves. Finding a custom slaughterer who will handle small batches of poultry is one option, but locating one who deals with ducks, which pose more of a plucking challenge than chickens do, can be difficult. You might want to find a pragmatic farmer or duck hunter who'd be willing to do the job in exchange for a share of the harvest.

## GETTING GOOD MEAT

Popular heavyweight breeds developed with meat production in mind include Muscovy, Pekin, Rouen, and Aylesbury ducks. Hybrids of Muscovies and Mallard-derivatives, called mule ducks or mulards, are also valued as meat birds, particularly in Europe. Ducks of the medium, lightweight, and bantam classes produce delicious meat, too—just not as much and at a slower rate than the heavyweights do. And these slower-growing birds tend to have less body fat as well (as already mentioned, Muscovies are also lean).

# Food Safety

Any raw or undercooked meat can harbor bacteria that proliferate under the right conditions and cause foodborne illness in humans. *Salmonella* bacteria, often linked to the consumption of improperly prepared eggs and poultry meats, cause diseases with extremely unpleasant symptoms, such as nausea, diarrhea, fever, and stomach cramps. For children and the elderly, these diseases can even be deadly. Adopt these safe handling tips to stay healthy:

• Thaw frozen duck in the refrigerator, in the microwave, or in cold water—never on the counter. Cook duck immediately after defrosting it.
• Use refrigerated duck within one to two days, or freeze it in its original packaging.

• When storing or handling duck or raw eggs, avoid cross-contamination with other foods. Use a separate cutting board for meats, and clean up and disinfect spills immediately.
• Never partially cook duck and refrigerate it to finish cooking later.
• Cook whole duck to an internal temperature of 165 degrees Fahrenheit (as measured with a meat thermometer). Refrigerate leftovers promptly.
• Cook eggs thoroughly before you eat them, and skip snacking on the cookie dough.
• Wash your hands with soap and warm water after handling raw meat and eggs.

*Source:* USDA Food Safety and Inspection Service

Ducklings raised for meat usually receive a starter or grower diet containing about 18 to 20 percent protein to promote speedy growth. They need ample water to drink and some water to bathe in. A meat duck such as the Pekin gains weight at lightning speed—nearly a pound a week—and will be ready for butchering in about eight to ten weeks, when it weighs approximately five pounds. Muscovies take longer to reach slaughter weight: about fourteen weeks. As with Cornish-cross broiler chickens, rapid growth in meat ducks often causes health problems and leg abnormalities; that's why ducks kept as pets, show birds, layers, or breeders should be switched to a lower protein diet after the first few weeks of life.

Remember that all ducks—even short-lived meat birds—benefit from having a spacious outdoor area where they can exercise, forage, and soak up the sunshine. Pasture-raised ducks won't grow as fast as confined birds will, but their meat is said to be tastier and healthier, with less fat and more heart-healthy omega-3 fatty acids.

## Selling Organic Meat and Eggs

The demand for organic foods, including poultry products, has seen amazing growth during the past twenty years or so as consumers have become more health-conscious and concerned about the ethical treatment of farm animals. In fact, the demand is so great and the number of organic operations so few that farmers making the switch to certified organic production often receive a premium for their products. If you plan to sell duck eggs and meat, making the leap to organic is worth considering.

As defined by the USDA, organic food is food that is produced in an environmentally responsible fashion, without the use of antibiotics, animal by-products, hormones, most conventional pesticides, synthetic fertilizers, or bioengineering. Producers planning to market their duck meat or eggs as organic must adhere to standards outlined in the USDA's National Organic Program. Organically raised poultry, for instance, must receive an organic diet from the second day of life onward and must have access to the outdoors. Organic certification by a USDA-accredited certification agency is currently required for farms that sell over $5,000 a year in organic agricultural products, whereas those making less are exempt. However, exempt operations must still conform to the standards in order to label their products as organic.

*This flock of ducks looks healthy and happy as they waddle across their sunny, spacious pasture. The exercise, fresh air and sunshine, and natural diet make for healthier ducks, and—according to many raisers—tastier meat and eggs.*

## Foie Gras

Foie gras (pronounced fwah-grah) is a French term for the fatty liver of geese and ducks, a delicacy first savored by the ancient Egyptians and still served in fancy restaurants today. According to the Humane Society of the United States, however, the commercial production of this expensive luxury food requires the cruel force-feeding of confined ducks and geese with a pressurized pump two to three times a day. This abnormally huge quantity of food makes the liver enlarge up to ten times its normal size, enough so that the birds find it difficult to move. Essentially, the organ becomes diseased. That's not a particularly appetizing thought, especially for those of us who try to treat our feathered friends as humanely as possible! The good news? More than a dozen countries have banned the production of foie gras.

Organic poultry production has its pros and cons. Certified organic feed costs more than conventional feed, and it can be difficult to locate. The road to organic certification involves submitting an application and farm management plan (plus a substantial fee), undergoing assessment and review by a certifier, and receiving an on-site inspection of your farm—a lengthy process that has to be repeated each year. Organic farmers cannot resort to as many quick fixes as conventional farmers can, such as using feed that contains preventive antibiotics or applying synthetic fertilizers to enhance pasture, so organic production tends to require more work, planning, and management than does conventional farming. For more information on the National Organic Program, including NOP Regulations and Guidelines, visit http://www.ams.usda.gov/nop/indexIE.htm.

But for those who have embraced it, organic poultry production has a payoff that goes beyond the higher prices many consumers will pay. Think about it for a moment: raising ducks this way requires organic feed, and the more the demand for organic feed grows, the more farmers will put additional land into organic production. That translates into fewer chemicals from synthetic pesticides, fertilizers, and herbicides contaminating the environment and affecting all its inhabitants—including us. Unfortunately, studies comparing organic with conventional poultry products are in short supply. But for organic food fans, it is enough to know that organic poultry receive a diet free of added inorganic arsenic (a cancer-causing agent) and antibiotics (which promote the development of drug-resistant bacteria); it seems intuitive to them that exposing their bodies to fewer artificial chemicals makes good health sense.

If converting to organic isn't a viable option for you, consider pasture or free-range duck farming. As mentioned before, eggs from pasture-reared poultry tend to taste and look better than eggs from confined birds. Meat from pastured birds usually has less fat and a

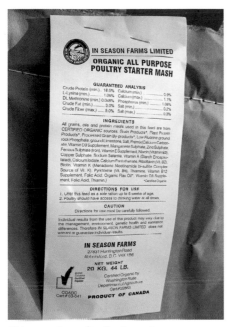

This organic poultry feed may be more expensive than conventional feed, but it's also free of added arsenic, antibiotics, and grains grown with applications of chemical fertilizers and pesticides.

firmer texture than does the meat of pen-potatoes. Some studies have shown lower cholesterol and higher levels of omega-3 fatty acids, vitamin E, and beta carotene in meat products from pastured birds. And from your duck's perspective, what could be better than having space to waddle around outside, gobbling slugs and snails, nibbling dandelions, and doing all the other things ducks are meant to do?

## DOWN AND FEATHERS

Duck down and feathers are the unavoidable—but incredibly useful—by-products of the butchering and plucking process. (And while on the subject of plucking—please, never live-pluck your ducks; it is painful for them.) Duck and goose down have long been used as warm and fluffy fillers for pillows, comforters, feather beds, ski jackets, and vests. If you've ever snuggled beneath a down comforter on a winter night, you'll know that when it comes to insulating you from the cold, nothing can outdo this remarkable natural product—as long as you keep it from getting wet.

Small flock raisers should count on this fluffy by-product of slaughter for personal—not commercial—use only; it would take years to collect enough down and small, soft feathers to create even one queen- or king-size comforter. A pillow might be a more reasonable goal!

As for those gorgeous duck feathers, you can clean, bag, and save them to use as cat toys, earrings, and quill pens, as well as for fly tying, painting, or other crafty projects.

This Muscovy female has lined her nest with a soft, insulating layer of down and small feathers. These by-products of the plucking process have long been used as fluffy filler for pillows, featherbeds, and comforters.

## Business Pointers

What our experts say about duck farming.

### Easier Plucking

"When processing our Muscovies, rather than go through the difficult process of waxing and plucking and dealing with the little dark pin feathers, we skin the breasts and use those. Muscovies have scrawny legs, which tend to dry out when you roast them, and most of my recipes call for duck breasts anyway. Skinning is so much faster and easier!"

*—Terry Ann Carkner*

### Processing Duck Eggs

"Our duck eggs are in high demand; we sell out very often. All of our ducks are pasture-ranged and organically fed. We scrub the eggs with baking soda to remove stains, debris, and odors, and inspect them for any cracks or pinholes made by the duck's toenails. This scrubbing—or any washing of the eggs—removes the natural protective oil layer on the shell's surface, called the bloom. When the eggs are dry, we re-oil or rebloom them with certified extra virgin olive oil. This extends the freshness of the eggs by several weeks. Duck eggs are wonderful to bake with since there is more protein in both the yolk and white, allowing the batter to rise magnificently; it adds a wonderful richness to the finished product. They can be eaten in the same ways as chicken eggs. The taste is determined by what the duck eats; since our ducks are fed layer feed, grasses, and bugs, they taste a lot like our chicken eggs, only richer."

*—Dawn Turbyfill*

### Going Organic

"Raising ducks 'all natural' or organically is pretty easy. The hardest part is finding certified organic feed; be prepared for a very pricey monthly feed bill. It does take time to even begin to recoup your expenditures. But within a year or two, word will travel about your beautiful birds and tasty eggs. A simple sign out front will keep you busy in a season or two."

*—Dawn Turbyfill*

## DUCK BUSINESSES

Wouldn't it be great to create a business around something you love, such as raising ducks? Raising ducks on a small scale won't make you rich. But if you live in the right area and have a knack for marketing, it's possible to turn a profit either by selling duck products—duck meat, eggs for eating and hatching, feathers, and down—or by selling ducks as pets, breeding stock, or exhibition stock. You don't have to put all your eggs in one basket, either: duck raising is perfectly compatible with other farm business enterprises, such as chicken operations, market gardens, community-supported agriculture, and orchards.

Don't leap into the duck business before you look, however. The demand for duck products is still much less than the demand for chicken and turkey products. Selling any food product for human consumption is a complicated affair, governed by a plethora of rules and regulations that vary from state to state. To find out what insurance, permits, and licenses are required or recommended for your intended business, start by checking with

*One of the ways you can profit from raising ducks is by selling ducklings for pets, layers, meat birds, breeders, or show stock.*

your state Department of Agriculture, your local health department, and your county extension office. You can locate them all in the white pages of your local phone book.

Devise a business plan, research your markets carefully, and start small, growing with your markets. Do you plan to sell eggs from your farm, at farmer's markets, or at both venues? Would you like to supply organic duck breasts to fancy restaurants or to grocery stores? Where will you advertise your hatching eggs and rare breed ducklings—via your Web site, Craigslist, the paper, or local feed stores? Internet marketing has become the norm for many small businesses. No matter how you plan to market your products, keep detailed records, or you'll never know whether your business enterprise is making or losing money.

Whatever you do with your little flock, above all have fun! You can bet that, given good care, your ducks will surely enjoy themselves in everything they do. After all, they're ducks!

# Acknowledgments

Heartfelt thanks go to the following people, who shared their advice, words of wisdom, time, and critiquing skills:

*Terry Ann Carkner* has raised Muscovies for five years. She and her husband, Dick, run Terry's Berries, an organic CSA (community-supported agriculture) farm on 20 acres near Tacoma, Washington. Her farm abounds with apple trees, raspberries, fresh and scrumptious vegetables, chickens, and—of course— slug-snacking Muscovy ducks. Visit her Web site at http://www.terrysberries.com.

*Howard Carroll* keeps Muscovy ducks and protects them from bald eagles on his fifteen-acre farm in Roy, Washington. A member of the American Farrier Association, he also runs Integrity Farrier Service.

*Cat Dreiling,* who has created a Web site for Muscovy enthusiasts called the Muscovy Duck Central, has kept ducks since she was nine years old. She currently raises Muscovies and Welsh Harlequin ducks (Silver and Gold phase) and sells hatching eggs and day-old ducklings from her farm in Deerfield, Kansas. Cat also raises sheep and is working to establish a flock of purebred Dorpers. You can find her Web site at http://www.muscovyduckcentral.com/thefarm/index.html.

*R. M. "Mick" Fulton, DVM, PhD*, is an associate professor of avian diseases at Michigan State University and a Diplomate of the American College of Poultry Veterinarians since 1992. He has served as an outside consultant to USAID on National Avian Influenza preparation for Rwanda, Africa.

*Dave Holderread* and his wife, Millie, raise more than forty-five waterfowl breeds and varieties at Holderread Waterfowl Farm & Preservation Center in Corvallis, Oregon. They specialize in bantam breeds, such as the Australian

Spotted and the East Indies, and also raise Silver Appleyard, Muscovy, Saxony, Ancona, Khaki Campbell, Cayuga, and Welsh Harlequin ducks. Dave, who has been passionate about ducks since childhood, is the author of *Storey's Guide to Raising Ducks* and *The Book of Geese.* Their Web site is http://www.holderreadfarm.com.

*Lou Horton,* of West Chicago, Illinois, has raised ducks and geese for almost forty years, including the beautiful black East Indies and the exotic Mandarin. He has served as a licensed waterfowl judge since 1970 and has won more than 100 championships in waterfowl at major shows all over the United States. As if all this weren't enough, he has written a monthly column on waterfowl for the past thirty years for the *Poultry Press.* Check out Lou's Web site, http://www.acornhollowbantams.com, one of the most useful and educational sites around on exhibition waterfowl.

*Bryon James* is the owner of Webster Road Feed in Graham, Washington. He has tended numerous ducklings over the years and keeps an assortment of ducks, chickens, peacocks, guinea fowl, and children on his small farm in Eatonville.

*Kate Morreale* named Golden Egg Farm in Hardwick, Massachusetts, for all the extra-special eggs produced there. She raises and sells hatching eggs from Show Quality Heritage and rare birds: white Aylesbury and black or white Indian Runner ducks, along with bantam Silky chickens in assorted colors. Kate is a member of the American Livestock Breeds Conservancy and the International Waterfowl Breeders Association. Admire her lovely pottery, poultry tiles, and birds at her Web site, http://www.goldeneggfarm.com.

*Jenifer Morrissey* runs Turkey Trot Rare Breeds at Willowtrail Farm in Gould, Colorado, where she raises Silver Appleyards and Anconas, along with beautiful Fell ponies. Of all the farm animals, she says, ducks are the happiest. Visit her Web site at http://www.willowtrailfarm.com.

*Melissa Peteler* is a former soil conservationist with the USDA. She now farms near Zumbrota, Minnesota, where she raises lamb and uses llamas to protect the grazing sheep from predators. She keeps Muscovy ducks because she can't help it. "Ducks are the embodiment of joy," says Melissa. "They seem impervious to most weather; rain is something to be enjoyed instead of avoided; every puddle is a treasure to be explored!" Melissa sells lamb and fiber through her Web site, http://www.risingmoonfarm.com.

*Angie Pilch* and her family have kept a mixed duck flock of Indian Runners, Khaki Campbells, and Blue Swedish for six years on Branonby Farms in Eatonville, Washington. They also keep and milk three friendly dairy goats.

*Trish Smith* and her family have delighted in Pekin ducks as personable pets for ten years, since their first imprinted duckling earned the name Soupy after it jumped in her daughter's bowl of vegetable soup. Trish tends a pair of slug-exterminating Pekins, along with horses, chickens, and assorted dogs and cats on her ten-acre farm in Graham, Washington.

*Dawn Turbyfill* was raised in a small farming community in Wisconsin, where her family had farmed for seven generations. Currently she raises rare breed ducks, chickens, turkeys, geese, Soay sheep, and cattle through Heirloom Heritage Farms (http://www.heirloom heritagefarms.com) and award-winning alpacas through Cedar Grove Alpacas (http://www.cedargrovealpacas.com). Dawn's husband, Robert, does most of the maintenance on their eight-acre farm in Spanaway, Washington, while Dawn shares her husbandry skills and love of animals with her three children (who are also starting businesses in livestock).

Abundant thanks to the following people for questions answered, pages proofread, and support provided: Sue Weaver; William Dean, PhD; Brett and Kelsey Langlois; Nada and Dorsey Hensley.

Thanks also to those at BowTie Inc. who offered me the opportunity to write this book: Karen Keb Acevedo and Art Stickney.

# Appendix A: Endangered Duck Breeds

Here's a rundown of thirteen duck breeds listed on the American Livestock Breed Conservancy's Conservation Priorities List and discussed in David Holderread's *Storey's Guide to Raising Ducks*. To learn more, contact the ALBC at 919-542-5704, or log on to http://www.albc-usa.org.

## CRITICAL

Fewer than 500 breeding birds in the United States, with five or fewer primary breeding flocks of fifty birds or more, and globally endangered:

**Ancona:** A hardy, all-purpose, medium-size breed developed in Great Britain and capable of laying more than 200 eggs a year. It possesses variable plumage of white mingled with lavender, black, silver, chocolate, or blue.

**Aylesbury:** A large, tame, fast-growing meat breed hailing from England. It has white plumage, white skin, and a long, pinkish-white bill. Lays fewer than 125 eggs a year.

**Magpie:** A light, active breed developed in Wales that can produce about 250 eggs annually. It flaunts white plumage with a black back and crown (color varieties include blues and silvers).

**Saxony:** A large, active, all-purpose duck from Germany that lays approximately 200 white eggs a year. Its plumage pattern resembles that of the Mallard, but its coloring is unique, with the drake sporting a bluish-gray head and back, and the female a buff color accented with creamy face stripes, neck, and belly.

**Silver Appleyard:** A sturdy, calm, dual-purpose breed native to England and developed by Reginald Appleyard. Lays more than 200 white eggs a year and sports silver-frosted, Mallard-like plumage, plus orange legs and feet.

**Welsh Harlequin:** A lightweight, streamlined Welsh breed that can produce more than 300 eggs a year and has a complicated plumage pattern similar to the wild Mallard.

## THREATENED

Fewer than 1,000 breeding birds in the United States, with seven or fewer primary breeding flocks, and globally endangered:

**Buff Orpington:** A medium, dual-purpose English duck that lays up to 200 eggs a year and grows fairly fast. Buff plumage.

**Cayuga:** A hardy, calm, medium-size breed developed in New York that lays 100 to 150 eggs a year. Its lovely feathers are black with a green iridescence.

## WATCH

Fewer than 5,000 breeding birds in the United States, with ten or fewer primary breeding flocks, and globally endangered:

**Campbell:** An energetic, lightweight English breed that can pump out a whopping 300-plus eggs annually. It comes in four varieties: Khaki, White, Dark, and Pied.

**Rouen:** Large, mellow meat duck originating in France that resembles the Mallard. It produces only about 35 to 125 eggs annually. The breed comes in standard and production types.

**Runner:** A lightweight, slender, active duck with a comical, upright carriage and long history in Asia. It can produce more than 200 white eggs annually.

**Swedish:** A stocky, medium utility breed developed in an area that was formerly part of the kingdom of Sweden. It lays 100 to 150 eggs and has slate blue plumage with a white bib. The drake's head is a darker blue than the female's.

## STUDY

Breeds of interest which either lack definition or lack genetic or historical documentation:

**Australian Spotted:** A rare, active, hardy bantam breed developed in the United States (not in Australia). It lays 50 to 125 eggs a year. The complicated plumage patterns of the three varieties include spotting on the body.

# Appendix B: Duck Diseases at a Glance

Although plenty of other nasty diseases circulate in the avian world, the following are the most common culprits affecting domestic duck flocks.

**Aspergillosis:** Moist bedding or feed makes a perfect medium for the growth of mold, including the fungus *Aspergillus,* whose spores can sicken ducks by promoting plaques in the air sacs and lungs. The spores most commonly spread in warm, dark places with high humidity. Aspergillosis is usually seen in ducklings; symptoms include lethargy and breathing troubles. Prevent this disease by tossing out moldy straw or feed, changing bedding regularly, and sanitizing your incubators as needed. Watch out for hardwood chips that contain bark.

**Avian influenza:** Avian influenza viruses are ubiquitous in many bird species around the world. Most of these virus strains are low pathogenic, causing little or no illness in affected birds. Highly pathogenic forms, however, can pass through a domestic poultry flock like lightning. Ducks often survive the highly pathogenic form of this disease without showing much in the way of clinical signs, but they can become avian influenza reservoirs, infecting chickens and other poultry. Ward off this disease with good biosecurity measures. Be especially careful to prevent contact between your flock and wild waterfowl.

**Avian (or Fowl) Cholera:** Although not transmitted as swiftly as avian influenza, avian cholera can also appear and spread through a flock in an explosive fashion. Symptoms of this bacterial disease include diarrhea, discharge from the mouth, appetite loss, labored breathing, and sudden death. Necropsy may reveal internal hemorrhage of the heart muscle and abdominal fat; an abnormally large, copper-colored liver; and an enlarged spleen. Unsanitary conditions and stagnant water contribute to this disease. Control rodents, which can also spread cholera, and dispose of dead animals promptly and properly.

**Colibacillosis (or *E. coli*):** A bacterium called *Escherichia coli* causes this common poultry infection, which can infect the yolk sac or cause a bacterial infection of the bloodstream in ducklings. Good sanitation procedures will help prevent this disease.

**Duck Viral Enteritis:** Also known by the frightening name of duck plague, this highly contagious disease caused by a type of herpes virus can infect waterfowl of any age. The virus is passed on by direct contact with infected birds or contaminated water. Symptoms include extreme thirst, nasal discharge, watery or bloody diarrhea, lethargy, drop in egg production, and ruffled feathers. Sadly, this disease can cause sudden death, with a high mortality rate, especially among older ducks. Necropsy of the bird will reveal internal hemorrhages and necrosis. Prevent contact between your ducks and wild waterfowl, which can carry the virus, and change footwear after being around wild waterfowl. Vaccines are available, but only on a limited basis.

**Duck Viral Hepatitis:** Like duck plague, this is an extremely contagious viral disease with a short incubation period that shows up suddenly and results in high mortality rates. The virus, which causes an enlarged, discolored liver, primarily strikes ducklings less than seven weeks old. Signs include lethargy, loss of balance, and spasmodic paddling movements of the feet; the duckling typically dies within an hour. To prevent this disease, keep ducklings isolated from older birds during the first five weeks, restrict access to wild waterfowl and their habitats, practice good hygiene, control rodents, and vaccinate breeder ducks to impart immunity to their ducklings. Knowing the breeder you acquire ducks from and his or her management methods can help you keep this disease off your farm.

**Riemerella (or Pasteurella) Anatipestifer Infection:** Also known by its much simpler name, new duck disease, this bacteria-caused illness mainly infects ducklings that are two to seven weeks of age. Signs may include discharge from the eyes and nasal openings, sneezing and coughing, sluggishness, head and neck tremors, weight loss, and a twisted neck. The disease can also cause sudden death. Providing clean drinking water and general good hygiene will help prevent the spread of this disease. A vaccine is also available.

# Glossary

**Aflatoxin**—various mycotoxins, or fungi toxins, produced by certain species of Aspergillus mold that can contaminate stored feeds and cause illness in ducks (and humans)

**Air cell**—an air pocket that forms in the large end of the egg after it is laid

**Albumen**—the white of an egg, consisting mainly of the protein albumin and water

**Altricial**—a term used to describe bird nestlings that are helpless, naked, and dependent on their parents to provide food and warmth

**Amino acids**—the basic building blocks of proteins

**Anemia**—a deficiency of oxygen-carrying red blood cells

**Anthelmintic**—an agent used to kill or eliminate internal parasites; also called dewormer

**Antibiotic**—a chemical substance that inhibits the growth of, or kills, bacteria and other micro-organisms

**Avian**—relating to, or characteristic of, birds

**Avian influenza**—a group of viruses found in many bird species around the world

**Aviary**—a large enclosure used to house birds

**Balut**—a delicacy enjoyed in Asia, consisting of a cooked, fertilized duck egg containing a partially developed embryo

**Bantam**—a variety or breed of fowl that is characterized by much smaller size than the original

**Biosecurity**—security measures taken to keep infectious diseases away from flock and farm, including quarantine, good sanitation, disinfectant foot baths, and rodent control

**Bloom**—the protective coating of an eggshell that keeps out pathogens

**Breed**—a group of animals selectively bred to possess certain desirable characteristics that distinguish it from another group; unlike species, breeds can produce fertile young when they mate

**Breeder ration**—feed given to breeding ducks to help them produce viable eggs

**Breeders**—ducks that are purposefully bred together to obtain fertile eggs or to produce ducklings

**Brooder**—a setup used to keep artificially reared ducklings warm and safe. It usually consists of a box, a light, a thermometer, food and water sources, and litter

**Broody**—a term for a duck or chicken that is eager to incubate its own eggs or those of another bird and hatch them out

**Bumblefoot**—a condition in which a duck's foot pads become cracked and infected; often caused by keeping birds on hard, dry surfaces or on wet, dirty litter

**Candling**—the process of checking an egg to determine whether it is fertile or viable by holding it up to a bright light

**Carbohydrates**—a group of organic compounds that serve as a major energy source in animal diets; include sugars, starches, and cellulose

**Caruncles**—the fleshy protuberances on a Muscovy's face and bill

**Cloaca**—the cavity into which a duck's intestinal, urinary, and reproductive tracts open

**Closed flock**—a flock maintained so that no new birds from outside the farm enter it and the resident birds remain on the farm at all times

**Clutch**—all the eggs deposited during a duck's laying cycle before she starts to set

**Coccidia**—an order of protozoans that parasitize many vertebrates

**Confinement**—management of livestock by keeping them exclusively in barns, houses, or pens

**Conformation**—the structure or form of an animal

**Contagious**—capable of being easily transmitted, as is the common cold; also, infectious

**Crop**—a pouch within the duck's esophagus that stores food for digestion

**Dabbling ducks, or dabblers**—ducks that tend to feed in shallow bodies of water by tipping and nibbling rather than by diving

**Drake**—a male duck

**Duck**—a member of the Anatidae family that is smaller than a goose or swan; also, a female duck

**Dummy egg**—an artificial or hard-boiled egg used as a substitute for a setting duck's own egg or to encourage laying birds to deposit their eggs in a certain spot

**Eclipse**—a post-breeding molt in which a drake acquires a drab plumage similar to that of a female duck

**Egg tooth**—a tiny, sharp projection on a hatching duckling's beak, used to peck through the shell; it is usually lost after hatching

**Epidermis**—the outermost layer of skin

**Feather**—an outgrowth of the epidermis unique to birds

**Fertile egg**—an egg that has been fertilized and is capable of producing a duckling

**Forage**—food sought by or fed to domestic animals; to look for one's own food

**Free range**—a system in which poultry or livestock are managed on pastures or permitted to forage outside rather than confined in barns or houses

**Gizzard**—a muscular chamber in the duck's lower stomach where food is ground, usually with the help of ingested grit; also called the ventriculus

**Grit**—granules of sand or fine stone consumed by ducks to help grind food in the gizzard

**Hatchability**—the hatching potential or viability of a fertile egg

**Hatching egg**—a fertile egg that is a good candidate for incubation; a fertile egg sold by hatcheries

**Hemorrhage**—profuse bleeding

**Humidity**—the amount of moisture in the air

**Hybrid**—the offspring of two animals of different species or breeds

**Hygrometer**—an instrument that measures humidity

**Imprinting**—a rapid learning process that takes place after birth, in which a duckling learns to recognize and become attracted either to another animal—usually its mother—or to an object

**Incubation**—the process of setting and hatching eggs, whether naturally or artificially

**Incubation period**—the time it takes for an egg to hatch once the female duck begins setting (or the egg is set within an incubator); also, the time it takes between infection and the appearance of a disease

**Incubator**—an apparatus used to hatch out eggs artificially; two common types are still-air and forced-air

**Infertile egg**—an egg that has not been fertilized

**Keel**—a fowl's breastbone, where the flight muscles attach

**Keratin**—the tough, fibrous protein that feathers, hair, and horn are made of

**Lamellae**—comblike plates lining a duck's upper and lower bill

**Layer**—a female duck kept for egg production

**Layer ration**—a feed formulated for poultry that are laying eggs. It provides the extra protein and calcium they need to produce a steady supply of eggs

**Litter**—bedding used for ducks, such as shavings or straw

**Maintenance ration**—a feed formulated for nonbreeding, nonlaying adult fowl; also called a holding or developer ration

**Molt**—the casting off and renewal of feathers in birds that occurs once or twice a year

**Monogamous**—having only one mate during the breeding season or breeding life of a pair

**Mutation**—a DNA change within an organism's genes that produces a new trait not found in the parents

**Necropsy**—an examination and dissection of a dead animal to discover the cause of death

**Necrosis**—the death of tissue or cells in a localized area of the body

**Omnivore**—an animal such as the duck that consumes both animals and plants

**Organic food**—food produced in an environmentally responsible fashion, without the use of antibiotics, hormones, conventional pesticides, synthetic fertilizers, and bioengineering

**Pandemic**—a disease epidemic that covers a large area

**Parasite**—an organism that lives in (endoparasite) or on (ectoparasite) another organism, the host, obtaining nutrients from the host but providing no benefit in return

**Pathogenic**—capable of causing disease, as in a pathogenic virus such as avian influenza

**Perching ducks**—ducks, such as the Muscovy and Wood duck, that perch and nest in trees

**Pin feathers**—new, growing feathers that are often filled with blood

**Pipping**—the drilling and pecking a duckling does to break out of its eggshell. An egg is pipped when you see that first little cracked spot on the shell

**Pneumatic**—containing air-filled cavities (for example, the bones of birds are pneumatic)

**Postnuptial molt**—the molting of feathers that usually occurs after the breeding season

**Precocial**—a term used to describe baby birds that are active, covered with down, and capable of feeding themselves and leaving the nest soon after hatching

**Preening**—a bird's grooming; it uses its beak to clean its feathers, distribute oil over them, and reposition them

**Premix**—a vitamin mixture that can be added to a combination of grains to create a nutritionally complete and balanced diet

**Primary feathers**—the large, outer flight feathers on each duck wing

**Proventriculus**—the duck's glandular stomach, which is located between crop and gizzard and secretes digestive enzymes

**Quarantine**—an isolation period imposed on an animal to prevent disease from spreading to other animals; also refers to the place where an animal is quarantined

**Raptor**—a bird of prey such as an eagle or hawk

**Safety area**—an enclosed area, having its own entrance and exit, that makes it easy for a person to enter or leave an aviary without letting the birds escape

**Salmonella**—bacteria in the genus *Salmonella* that can cause foodborne illness in humans and other mammals

**Secondary feathers**—the inner row of flight feathers on each wing

**Setting**—the act of incubating eggs or sitting on a nest

**Species**—a natural population of animals that interbreeds and lives in reproductive isolation from another population

**Speculum**—a wing patch on the secondary wing feathers, common in ducks

**Starter ration**—a high-protein feed formulated for ducklings to eat during their first few weeks

**Strain**—a group of birds within a breed or variety, often developed by one breeder

**Trait**—a genetically determined distinguishing characteristic (for example, plumage color)

**Twisted wing**—a condition in waterfowl characterized by the primary wing feathers growing up and away from the bird's body; also called angel wing

**Uropygial gland**—a gland located at the base of the duck's tail feathers; also known as the preen gland or oil gland, it secretes an oil that the duck uses in preening its feathers

**Variety**—a category within a species or breed (the White Call, for example, is a variety of Call duck)

**Vent**—the external cloacal opening in birds

**Ventriculus**—see *Gizzard*

**Vertebrate**—an animal that possesses a backbone, or spinal column

**Waterfowl**—water birds, particularly ducks, swans, and geese

**Yolk**—the central yellow part of an egg that provides nutrients to the developing embryo

**Zoonotic disease**—an animal disease that can be passed to humans

# Resources

## ONLINE RESOURCES

How did we ever get by before the Internet? Whether you're looking for day-old ducklings, an incubator, information on waterfowl diseases, or a duck forum to frequent, you'll find it online. We've weeded through all the chicken-biased poultry sites out there to bring you the best resources for raisers of small duck flocks.

## HATCHERIES AND BREEDERS

A number of these hatcheries also offer poultry supplies and books.

### Cackle Hatchery (Missouri)

http://www.cacklehatchery.com
417-532-4581
In business since 1936, Cackle Hatchery markets regular and rare duck breeds, including Ancona, Cayuga, Runner, Pekin, Rouen, Khaki Campbell, and Welsh Harlequin ducklings. Check out their Web site for photos of the different breeds, adults as well as ducklings; some supplies; and a six ducks/four geese waterfowl special.

### C. M. Estes Hatchery, Inc. (Missouri)

http://www.esteshatchery.com
417-862-3593
Established in 1922, C. M. Estes Hatchery sells ducklings from a delightful array of breeds: White Pekin, Rouen, Mallard, Fawn Runner, Khaki Campbell, Ancona, Swedish, Cayuga, Crested, and Welsh Harlequin.

### DuckEggs.com

http://www.duckeggs.com
909-287-3505
Duckeggs.com specializes in selling fresh eating or hatching eggs, mainly from Pekins and Mallards. You can also order an incubator/hatching egg package.

## Hoffman Hatchery, Inc. (Pennsylvania)

http://www.hoffmanhatchery.com

717-365-3694

Hoffman Hatchery started in 1948 with one small incubator; today, it hatches several thousand eggs a week during the main hatching season. The duckling selection includes White Muscovies, Pekins, Rouen, Indian Runners, Swedish, Cayuga, Welsh Harlequin, and Mallards. It also carries a good selection of brooding supplies, feeders, waterers, incubators, and other poultry equipment.

## Holderread Waterfowl Farm & Preservation Center (Oregon)

http://www.holderreadfarm.com

541-929-5338

With one of the best waterfowl collections in the world, Dave and Millie Holderread specialize in quality purebred ducks and geese for exhibition, meat and egg production, and breeding stock. They offer ducklings and adults of many beautiful rare breeds and varieties, including Australian Spotted, Saxony, Magpie, Dutch Hook Bill, and Runners (eight varieties). You can also order various duckling assortments.

## Metzer Farms (California)

http://www.metzerfarms.com

800-424-7755

This family-owned operation has been hatching ducks and geese since 1978. They ship a variety of day-old ducklings, including Pekin, Rouen, Cayuga, Buff Orpington, Blue Swedish, Mallard, Runners in several varieties, and a few high-producing hybrids. These folks also market eating eggs and blown-out duck eggs for decorating. Along with their selection of waterfowl books and feeds, you'll find a handy duck starter kit with water fountain, feeder, brooder lamp, and more.

## Murray McMurray Hatchery (Iowa)

http://www.mcmurrayhatchery.com

800-456-3280

Billing itself as the world's largest rare breed hatchery, this company sells hatching duck eggs and Runner, Blue Swedish, Buff Orpington, Mallard, Cayuga, Khaki Campbell, Rouen, and Pekin ducklings. You can order various mixed packages of ducklings, chicks, turkeys, and geese. It also offers ornamental Wood ducks and Mandarins. McMurray carries an assortment of poultry supplies, including organic feeds, incubators, disinfectants, and books.

## Sand Hill Heirloom Seeds & Poultry Preservation Center (Iowa)

http://www.sandhillpreservation.com

563-246-2299

A small family farm working to save our planet's genetic diversity, Sand Hill Preservation Center offers Magpie, Dutch Hookbill, Campbell, Golden Cascade, Runner, and other ducklings, plus breed assortments. It also specializes in heirloom seeds.

## Seven Oaks Game Farm (North Carolina)

http://www.poultrystuff.com

910-791-5352

Want Call ducks? Seven Oaks Game Farm has fourteen different color varieties to choose from. You'll also find wild Mallards, Pekins, Muscovies, and Runners. Check out their online catalog filled with incubators, brooders, cage-building supplies, watering systems, books, and other poultry and game bird necessities.

## Stromberg's Chicks & Gamebirds Unlimited (Minnesota)

http://www.strombergschickens.com

800-720-1134 (orders only)

Stromberg's vast selection of poultry supplies will blow your mind. It carries nest boxes, aviary netting, shade panels, incubators, brooders, water heaters, and lots more. It also sells a diverse collection of ornamental, regular, and fancy duck breeds, including Ancona, Harlequin, Swedish, Mallard, Cinnamon Teal, Mandarin, Wood duck, Aylesbury, Muscovy, and exhibition Rouen. Check out its list of waterfowl books, too.

## POULTRY SUPPLIES

### Dakota Nesting Structures (North Dakota)

http://www.dakotanestingstructures.com

701-845-5457

This company markets artificial nesting structures for Mallards, Wood ducks, and geese, as well as feeders. While pri-marily intended for birds in the wild, these products could be useful in an aviary or pond setting.

## EggCartons.com (Massachusetts)

http://www.eggcartons.com

If you plan to sell eggs, check out this site: EggCartons.com offers egg car-tons, trays, shipping cases, incubators, and other poultry supplies.

## Jeffers Livestock (Alabama)

http://www.jefferslivestock.com

800-533-3377

Although Jeffers' poultry vaccines and medications are geared toward chick-ens, you'll find waterers, feeders, incuba-tors, and remedies that can be used for ducks, along with plenty of fencing and farm essentials. Better yet, the prices at Jeffers can't be beaten!

## Poultryman's Supply Company (Kentucky)

http://www.poultrymansupply.com

859-745-4944

Check out Poultryman's stock of incuba-tors, brooders, feeders and waterers, egg cartons, and more.

## Smith Poultry & Game Bird Supply (Kansas)

http://www.poultrysupplies.com

913-879-2587

Smith Poultry & Game Supply carries a wide range of useful poultry supplies, including incubators, brooders, range feed-ers, processing equipment, and netting.

## ORGANIZATIONS AND CLUBS

Joining an organization or club is a wonderful way to network with and learn from other duck enthusiasts, breeders, and exhibitors.

### American Bantam Association (ABA) (New Jersey)

http://www.bantamclub.com
973-383-8633

Representing bantam chicken and duck breeders since 1914, the ABA fosters the breeding, exhibition, and sale of purebred bantam poultry, including bantam ducks. Peruse its Web site for message board, membership information, and savvy articles about biosecurity.

### The American Livestock Breeds Conservancy (ALBC) (North Carolina)

http://www.albc-usa.org
919-542-5704

The ALBC, based in Pittsboro, North Carolina, has worked since 1977 to conserve and maintain the genetic diversity of nearly 100 endangered livestock breeds. Visit its wonderful site to check out detailed breed profiles, conservation priority status, and photos of threatened livestock, including thirteen duck breeds. You can also shop for livestock books and learn how you can help the cause.

### American Poultry Association (APA) (Pennsylvania)

http://www.amerpoultryassn.com
724-729-3459

The APA, founded in 1873, promotes and protects the standardbred poultry industry, encourages poultry shows, and publishes the American Standard of Perfection, which lists and describes all recognized purebred poultry breeds (including ducks) and varieties. Surf its site to find out how to join and obtain show, exhibitor, and poultry health information.

### British Waterfowl Association (BWA) (UK)

http://www.waterfowl.org.uk

The BWA is dedicated to the keeping, breeding, and conservation of all waterfowl, including domestic ducks. Click on "Domestic Waterfowl" and then "BWA Information Leaflets" to find concise information on breeds, ailments, pond construction, and plenty more. It also maintains breeder and book lists.

### Call Duck Association UK (CDA) (Wales)

http://www.callducks.net

The CDA promotes the health and welfare of the adorable Call duck. Its site contains the breed's interesting history, along with general management advice.

### Domestic Waterfowl Club of Great Britain (UK)

http://www.domestic-waterfowl.co.uk/

This club promotes the breeding, showing, and sheer enjoyment of purebred waterfowl. Its site is a must-see, brimming with breed descriptions and great photos, plus fact sheets on waterfowl health problems, information on incubation and rearing, and much more. Want to know what all those Call color varieties look like? You'll find pictures here.

## International Waterfowl Breeders Association (IWBA)

http://www.crohio.com/IWBA
Formed by waterfowl breeder and judge Lou Horton in 1971, the IWBA offers a master exhibitor program and publishes a quarterly newsletter with articles on breeding, raising, and showing waterfowl. Check the Web site for information on joining and meets, and don't forget to look at the Breed of the Month.

## National Call Breeders of America

http://www.callducks.org
This organization, started in 1986, encourages the exhibition of the diminutive Call duck. At its Web site, you'll find a list of breeders, descriptions of Call duck varieties, a mentorship program, and helpful articles on breeding and on the condition called bumblefoot.

## Society for the Preservation of Poultry Antiquities (SPPA)

http://www.feathersite.com/Poultry/SPPA/SPPA.html
570-837-3157
The SPPA's admirable goal is to perpetuate and improve rare poultry breeds, including ducks. It also sponsors awards and shows. Check out the interesting articles on its Web site, including information on avian influenza and a position paper on the National Animal ID System.

## DUCK FEED SUPPLIERS

### Hubbard Feeds

http://www.hubbardfeeds.com
Markets Tradition duck and goose feeds.

### Mazuri

http://www.mazuri.com
This company supplies zoos with formulated fare for a wide variety of animals. It offers several ornamental waterfowl diets.

### Zeigler

http://www.zeiglerfeed.com
Zeigler's Sinking Duck Breeder diet is a balanced waterfowl diet designed to reduce wastage.

## UNIVERSITY RESOURCES

Loads of university and extension sites out there offer poultry information; unfortunately, in this case, "poultry" usually refers to chickens and turkeys. For information geared toward our web-footed poultry, visit the following sites:

## Cornell University Duck Research Laboratory

http://www.duckhealth.com
This site has a wealth of information on basic duck care, including nutrition, housing, and egg incubation. A federally

licensed biologics production facility, the Duck Laboratory also sells vaccines for common duck diseases and has a diagnostic laboratory service.

## Oklahoma State University Breeds of Livestock

http://www.ansi.okstate.edu/poultry/ducks/index.htm

This site contains photos, brief histories, and descriptions of ten domestic duck breeds, including the lovely Cayuga and interesting Muscovy.

## University of California— Cooperative Extension

Muscovy Duck Care Practices
http://animalscience.ucdavis.edu/Avian/muscovy1001.htm

Although this guide focuses on raising Muscovies on a large commercial scale, it contains detailed information on general care, the rearing of ducklings, and Muscovy health that would be helpful to any duck raiser. Don't skip the in-depth section on biosecurity measures—a practice more important than ever before with the growing threat of avian influenza.

## University of Minnesota Extension Service

http://www.extension.umn.edu

On the left-hand side, click on Farm, then Poultry (under the Livestock heading). You'll find some information on raising ducks, preventing salmonella in poultry flocks, and processing poultry at home.

## Virginia Cooperative Extension

http://www.ext.vt.edu/resources

To get to small flock information that includes waterfowl, be prepared to do some clicking: First click on the cow icon that says Livestock, Poultry & Dairy; then hit Poultry, followed by Small Specialty Flock, and finally Management Requirements. Here, you'll find helpful fact sheets on waterfowl management requirements, brooding fowl, the raising of fowl in urban areas, and more.

## OTHER USEFUL WEB SITES

Informative, fascinating, or just plain fun: the following quacking good Web sites are worth a visit.

## Acorn Hollow Bantams

http://acornhollowbantams.com/

Lou Horton, a waterfowl judge and bantam duck breeder, has packed his site with excellent articles on the care of exhibition waterfowl; subjects include housing, hatching waterfowl eggs, natural incubation, exhibition, and much more. He also offers breeding stock for sale.

## Animal Welfare Institute

http://www.animalwelfare.com/farm/standards/ducks.htm

Visit this page to read the Animal Welfare Institute's Approved Welfare Standards for ducks. The institute's worthy goal is to reduce the pain and fear inflicted on animals by people and to promote alternative farming systems over factory farming.

## Ashton Waterfowl (UK)

http://www.ashtonwaterfowl.net

This site features photos and information on bantam ducks, especially Calls. The Ashtons, authors of *The Domestic Duck,* have bred waterfowl for more than twenty-five years.

## ATTRA, National Sustainable Agriculture Information Service

http://www.attra.ncat.org

The ATTRA site, created and managed by the National Center for Appropriate Technology, contains a treasure trove of helpful articles and information on a wide range of farming topics. Self-reliance and sustainable agriculture are the goals here. For poultry, click on Livestock, then click Poultry.

## The Coop

http://www.the-coop.org

Dedicated to those who breed, raise, and show poultry, waterfowl, and game birds, the Coop offers small flock owners a forum for discussion on a wide variety of poultry topics, including waterfowl. The site also features a marketplace and links to poultry articles.

## Centers for Disease Control and Prevention (CDC)

http://www.bt.cdc.gov

Avian influenza isn't a pleasant topic, but it's one all duck raisers should educate themselves about. The CDC maintains an informative, up-to-date page on avian influenza. Look under Recent Outbreaks & Incidents and click on Avian flu.

## Eggbid.com

http://www.eggbid.com

At this online auction site for poultry enthusiasts you can bid on ducks, duck eggs, books, all manner of poultry supplies, and collectibles. Neat!

## FeatherSite

http://www.feathersite.com

This cool site for avian enthusiasts has lots of duck breed photos and helpful links. Scroll down for a list of poultry books, including books on waterfowl and pond construction.

## Live Ducks

http://www.liveducks.com

Lori and Greg Goodman's tremendously fun site is a great resource for pet duck owners and boasts the only 24/7 duck webcam on the net. You'll find duck news, entertaining stories, breed photos, and loads of helpful information.

## The Merck Veterinary Manual, Ninth Edition

http://www.merckvetmanual.com

If you can handle the scientific jargon, this easy-to-search online edition of the animal health reference book that veterinarians have relied on since 1955 contains a wealth of information about poultry diseases and health conditions. Disease entries outline clinical signs, diagnosis criteria, and prevention and treatment strategies.

## Muscovy Duck Central

http://www.muscovyduckcentral.com
Muscovy lovers who visit this site can join in the forum, peruse the classifieds, and check the breeders' list.

## The Muscovy Duck Group

http://groups.msn.com/muscovyduck group
This site hosts a worldwide community of Muscovy enthusiasts and contains message boards, a breeders' list, and photos of Muscovy varieties, both adult birds and ducklings.

## The National Organic Program (NOP)

http://www.ams.usda.gov/NOP
If you want to sell organic eggs or meat, the USDA's National Organic Program site has the entire scoop on regulations and rules.

## The New Agrarian

http://www.newagrarian.com
David Walbert's entertaining and informative site (click on the duck picture) describes how he manages his little flock of Khaki Campbells on a daily basis and offers some great duck-raising advice. Be sure to check out his duckling diary, so you know what you're in for.

## New South Wales (NSW) Department of Primary Industries (Australia)

http://www.agric.nsw.gov.au/reader/ poultry

Click on Duck raising to bring up an informative publication that covers duck breeds, disease control, housing design, egg production, brooding and rearing ducklings, nutrition, and more.

## Northwest Wildfowl

http://www.greatnorthern.net/~dye/
This farm/sanctuary in Washington, created by aviculturists Paul and Lynn Dye, is home to more than fifty species of ornamental wild waterfowl and grouse. At its Web site, the late Paul Dye has left a legacy of valuable information on different ornamental waterfowl species as well as on getting started in aviculture.

## The Pet Duck and Goose Association

http://www.geocities.com/petduckasso ciation/
Ducks in the house? It's no joke— some people have welcomed ducks into their homes and cars, as well as their hearts. This site gives information on house ducks, duck diapers, and more, as well as offering entertaining accounts of house and traveling ducks.

## The Poultry Connection

http://www.poultryconnection.com
Learn and share with other duck raisers at the general waterfowl forum hosted at this site.

## USDA Food Safety and Inspection Service

http://www.fsis.usda.gov/Fact_Sheets/
Click on Poultry Preparation and then

Duck and Goose from Farm to Table to learn safe meat-handling and cooking strategies that will ward off salmonella and other nasties.

## World Health Organization (WHO)

http://www.who.int/en

If you dare to learn more about highly pathogenic avian influenza and its spread, this site provides the latest information. Click on Avian Influenza—Full coverage in the top right-hand corner of the home page.

## RECOMMENDED READING

As far as I'm concerned, the computer will never replace a good book (or magazine) for curling up with on a rainy day. Alas, duck books are pretty rare compared to chicken books; keep an eye out for these treasures.

## BOOKS

Ashton, Chris and Mike. *The Domestic Duck.* Crowood Press, 2001.

The Ashtons, who have raised waterfowl in Great Britain for more than twenty-five years, have traced the origins of the country's twenty-three standardized duck breeds. You'll also find information on keeping and breeding these delightful birds.

Bartlett, Tom. *Ducks and Geese: A Guide to Management.* Crowood Press, 1986.

This little book offers a practical introduction to keeping ducks and geese,

based on this British waterfowl breeder's own management techniques. His last chapter on how he manages his collection throughout the seasons has some very helpful advice.

Damerow, Gail. *Barnyard in Your Backyard: A Beginner's Guide to Raising Chickens, Ducks, Geese, Rabbits, Goats, Sheep and Cattle.* Storey Publishing, 2002. Damerow devotes pages 63 through 114 of this book to ducks and geese, giving a concise overview of some commonly kept breeds, basic care of these breeds, breeding, health issues, and products. A big bonus: she's probably got your other farm animals covered, too.

Holderread, Dave. *Storey's Guide to Raising Ducks.* Storey Publishing, 2001. This information-packed, 315-page book is the duck raiser's bible, a must-have for both novice and experienced raiser. Author Dave Holderread condenses more than forty years of experience raising ducks, offering tried-and-true advice on duck care and management, breeding, feeds, and health. You'll also find an excellent chapter on duck genetics and colors, along with in-depth breed profiles. If you want to try concocting your own duck feed, be sure to check out his formulations.

Johnsgard, Paul A. *Ducks, Geese, and Swans of the World.* University of Nebraska Press, 1978.

This comprehensive and out-of-print reference classic deserves a spot of honor in the library of anyone who loves wild, ornamental waterfowl. It's packed with fascinating natural history on the entire Anatidae family and features detailed black-and-white illustrations. Look for a used copy on eBay.

National Research Council. *Nutrient Requirements of Poultry.* National Academies Press, 1994.
Good nutrition is essential to the health of our duck flocks. Learn all about this somewhat complicated subject within the pages of this in-depth classic book on poultry nutrition, newly revised in 1994. It even has a chapter devoted specifically to duck nutrition. Warning: contains scientific jargon.

Raiethel, Heinz-Sigurd and Julie R. Mancini. *The Duck Handbook.* Barron's Press, 2005.
This lovely, easy-to-read book focuses on ornamental ducks, but most of the information applies to the care of domestic utility ducks as well. It's chock full of concise and interesting facts about duck behavior; species and breed descriptions; and advice on housing, nutrition, and more. The color photos are gorgeous.

## PERIODICALS
*Backyard Poultry*
http://www.backyardpoultrymag.com
This bimonthly poultry magazine is packed with practical management information and advice. Although it focuses primarily on chickens, you'll find occasional articles on waterfowl.

*The Game Bird Gazette*
http://www.gamebird.com
This color magazine covers the keeping and raising of ducks, along with other game birds like quail, pheasant, peacocks, and doves.

*Hobby Farms*
http://www.hobbyfarmsmagazine.com
This bimonthly magazine covers a wide range of informative topics of interest to small-farm owners.

*Poultry Enthusiast Magazine*
http:// www.poultryenthusiast.com
You'll learn plenty about maintaining small poultry flocks—including ducks—within the pages of this full-color bimonthly magazine. Read about nutrition, health, genetics, housing, and more.

*Poultry Press*
http://www.poultrypress.com
Promoting standardbred poultry since 1914, the family-owned Poultry Press brings you photos and information on show winners, articles on all types of poultry, classified ads, and more each month. Plus, each issue comes with a Buy Two, Get One Free coupon for a bag of Purina Mills feed. Cool! Order a sample issue online, and check out their image gallery of duck breeds.

# Index

# ABOUT THE AUTHOR

**Cherie Langlois** is a freelance writer and photographer who specializes in farm, pet, and travel topics. She's had more than 150 articles published and is a contributing editor to *Hobby Farms* magazine. A former zookeeper and veterinary assistant with a BA in zoology, Cherie has worked with a variety of waterfowl and has raised Muscovy ducks on her five-acre farm in Washington state for fifteen years. Her much-loved menagerie, managed with the help of husband Brett and daughter Kelsey, also includes horses, sheep, goats, chickens, cats, a dog, a house rabbit, and a cockatiel. She can be reached at langlois@blarg.net.